ATTACHMENT STYLES AS A PREDICTOR OF EMOTIONAL INTELLIGENCE IN A U.S. POPULATION

By
Titilola Ologbonjaiye

Dr. Kelly Schmitt, Chair
Dr. Richard Mendelson, Committee Member
Dr. Shoshana Dayanim, Committee Member

Dr. Ashlee Robertson, Dean of the Graduate School
Keiser University Graduate School-Psychology

A Dissertation in
Partial Fulfillment
of the Requirements
for the Degree
Doctor of Philosophy

Keiser University
October 2024

ATTACHMENT STYLES AS A PREDICTOR OF EMOTIONAL INTELLIGENCE IN A U.S. POPULATION

ATTACHMENT STYLES AS A PREDICTOR OF EMOTIONAL INTELLIGENCE IN A U.S. POPULATION

By

Titilola Ologbonjaiye

October 2024

APPROVED:

____

Dr. Kelly Schmitt. Faculty Mentor and Chair

____

Dr. Richard Mendelson, Committee Member

____

Dr. Shoshana Dayanim, Committee Member

ACCEPTED AND SIGNED:

____

Laurie Slifka, PhD

Chair, Psychology Program

____

Ashlee Robertson, PhD

Dean, Graduate School

Abstract

This study explores the extent to which attachment styles can predict emotional intelligence among U.S. college students. Utilizing the emotional quotient inventory 2.0 (EQ-i 2.0) to measure emotional intelligence, which includes subscales for stress management, self-perception, interpersonal skills, self-expression, and decision-making, the study employed the RSQ to assess attachment styles, encompassing secure, dismissive, preoccupied, and fearful categories. Additionally, a comprehensive review of the interactions between these two variables was conducted. The findings indicate that attachment styles can predict a person's emotional intelligence in a linear and positive manner. However, these results differ slightly from those of the study by Hamarta et al. (2009), potentially due to variations in participant demographics or the emotional intelligence instruments and subscales employed. Exploratory analysis revealed interactions between emotional intelligence and attachment style based on gender, age, and race. Overall, this study contributes to the limited body of research on the predictive relationship between attachment styles and emotional intelligence.

Dedication

This dissertation is dedicated to my family. First and foremost, pursuing my education goals would not have been possible without the encouragement and support of my husband, Christopher Ologbonjaiye. He is the best partner one could hope for, and over the past several years, he has taken on many tasks so I could focus on my studies. Our beautiful children and grandchildren motivate and inspire me every day. I look forward to watching them grow and achieve their exciting milestones and accomplishments. A special thank you goes out to my mother, Arinola Abigail Sanni. She taught me to dream big and never give up on achieving my goals. Lastly, thanks to my siblings and friends; whenever I need extra help or a listening ear, I know I can count on them, and I am forever grateful.

Acknowledgments

I want to express my sincere gratitude to my dissertation chair, Dr. Kelly Schmitt. She guided me through the dissertation process with patience and kindness. Without her invaluable counsel, this work would not have been possible. I also want to acknowledge my committee members, Dr. Richard Mendelson and Dr. Shoshana Dayanim. I enjoyed being a student in Dr. Dayanim's classes and have learned much from her. Dr. Richard was gracious enough to join the committee later in the process with his expertise in Emotional Intelligence, and I am thankful for his encouragement and advice. Lastly, I also want to thank Dr. Laurie Slifka, who was on my dissertation committee at the beginning of this process. A special acknowledgment goes out to the participants in this study. Thank you for your time and openness while sharing your experiences.

Table of Contents

xii

Chapter 1. Introduction

Understanding the intricate interplay between emotional intelligence and attachment styles is not just a pursuit for psychologists and scholars—it is a crucial exploration for anyone seeking to enhance the quality of human connection and mental well-being. Regarding emotional intelligence, individuals emerge as reflective thinkers, their interactions with the world and others becoming windows into their unique approaches to achieving goals (Bar-On et al., 2000). Delving into this dynamic connection holds profound implications for addressing a spectrum of behavioral and mental health disorders, from mild to moderate manifestations of internalizing symptomatology like depression, stress, and anxiety. Unraveling the intricate web of emotional intelligence and attachment styles unveils strategies to nurture prosocial behaviors, potentially correcting and enhancing an individual's emotional and relational framework. In this context, improving emotional intelligence could be the key to reshaping an individual's attachment style, opening new avenues for transformative change.

Background of Study

This study aims to replicate and build upon the findings of Hamarta et al. (2009), specifically exploring the predictive relationship between attachment styles and emotional intelligence. Notably, most existing studies are based on either attachment style or emotional intelligence, needing a comprehensive examination of their interconnected dynamics. Grounded in the assumptions articulated by Bar-On et al. (2000), this study posits that human behaviors are purposeful and goal-oriented and influenced by active engagement with the environment.

Additionally, it draws on the idea that individuals possess multiple behavioral systems that evolved because of the need for survival, as elucidated by Ainsworth (1978). The concept of behavioral systems suggests that predictable behaviors are influenced by both external and internal factors, with effect and emotions playing crucial roles in shaping responses.

Emphasizing the significance of social bonding, nature, and the intricate interplay of emotions in mental states, physiology, and interpersonal engagement (Johnson, 2018), this study adopts an objective and holistic approach to understanding individuals based on their attachment styles. Johnson (2018) argues that such an approach empowers individuals and opens avenues for transformative change by leveraging the attachment system. For instance, addressing insecurities in therapy by acknowledging an insecure attachment can lead to profound positive shifts when met with acceptance and reassurance.

This study builds on the assertion by Hamarta et al. (2009) that emotional intelligence can be predicted based on attachment style, contending that these components are interconnected and develop over time, with attachment styles originating in early childhood through caregiver interactions. The developmental nature of emotional intelligence is recognized, and this research underscores the need to educate caregivers on fostering secure attachments in early life, ultimately contributing to higher emotional intelligence in individuals. By exploring how attachment styles accurately predict emotional intelligence, this study aims to deepen our understanding of the fundamental elements that shape human interactions and psychological well-being.

Statement of the Problem

The current study seeks to address the pressing issue of understanding the relationship between emotional intelligence (EI) and attachment styles in United States students, building upon the findings of Hamarta et al. (2009) through research conducted with Turkish students. The research problem revolves around determining the existence and extent of a significant relationship between emotional intelligence and attachment style subscales. This research study investigates whether individuals scoring high or low in emotional intelligence exhibit distinct attachment style patterns and vice versa. The research conducted by the National Institute of Mental Health (2017) showed that 20% of Americans live with mental illness. 50 to 60% of people have a secure attachment style (Belot et al., 2021). 64% of people show low emotional intelligence and unlabeled emotions are misunderstood, leading to irrational choices and counterproductive actions (Legacy Place).

Furthermore, the study will explore the potential moderating effects of age, gender, and race on the relationship between emotional intelligence and attachment styles. The primary objective is to contribute valuable insights into the practical applications of emotional intelligence and attachment-style interventions, particularly in correcting behavior problems. Mental health workers may benefit from this research by understanding how improving attachment styles could enhance emotional intelligence, informing targeted therapeutic approaches for individuals with emotional dysregulation.

Purpose of the Study

The primary objective of the present study is to investigate the relationship between attachment styles and emotional intelligence among United States students. Specifically, we aim to explore how variations in attachment styles, including secure, dismissive, preoccupied, and fearful, are associated with emotional intelligence and its subscales—stress management, self-perception, self-expression, interpersonal, and decision-making.

Rationale

Understanding the intricate interplay between attachment styles and emotional intelligence is crucial for elucidating the factors contributing to an individual's mental well-being and interpersonal relationships. By identifying how specific attachment styles relate to distinct aspects of emotional intelligence, such as stress management, self-perception, self-expression, interpersonal skills, and decision-making, this study seeks to provide valuable insights for mental health professionals, educators, and researchers. The rationale behind examining these variables lies in the potential impact on developing targeted interventions, ultimately fostering emotional well-being and enhancing individuals' abilities to navigate various social and emotional challenges. The study's findings may contribute to a broader understanding of the connections between attachment styles and emotional intelligence, offering practical implications for improving psychological health and interpersonal functioning.

Research Questions and Hypotheses

The present study's independent variable (IV) is attachment style and the attachment style subscales: secure, dismissive, preoccupied, and fearful. The present study's dependent variable (DV) is the Emotional Intelligence and Emotional Intelligence subscales: stress management, self-perception, self-expression, interpersonal, and decision-making.

The research questions and hypotheses are:

Research Question 1: Is there a significant positive correlation between secure attachment style as measured by RSQ (Griffin & Batholomew, 1994) and emotional intelligence (Stress Management, Self -Perception, Self-Expression, Interpersonal, and decision-making) as measured by EQ2.0-I (Bar-On, 1997)?

> Hypothesis 1a (null): Secure attachment style is not positively related to the self- perception subscale of emotional intelligence.
>
> Hypothesis 1a (alternative): Secure attachment style is positively related to the self- perception subscales of emotional intelligence.
>
> Hypothesis 1b (null): Secure attachment style is not positively related to the self- expression subscale of emotional intelligence.

Hypothesis 1b (alternative): Secure attachment style is positively related to the self- expression subscales of emotional intelligence.

Hypothesis 1c (null): Secure attachment style is not positively related to the interpersonal subscale of emotional intelligence.

Hypothesis 1c (alternative): Secure attachment style is positively related to the interpersonal subscales of emotional intelligence.

Hypothesis 1d (null): Secure attachment style is not positively related to the decision-making subscale of emotional intelligence.

Hypothesis 1d (alternative): Secure attachment style is positively related to the Decision-Making subscales of emotional intelligence.

Hypothesis 1e (null): Secure attachment style is not positively related to the stress management subscale of emotional intelligence.

Hypothesis 1e (alternative): Secure attachment style is positively related to the stress management subscales of emotional intelligence.

Research Question 2: Is there a significant correlation between Dismissive attachment style as measured by RSQ (Griffin & Batholomew, 1994) and emotional intelligence subscales (Stress Management, Self - Perception, Self-Expression, Interpersonal, and decision-making) as measured by EQ2.0-I (Bar-On, 1997)?

Hypothesis 2a (null): Dismissive attachment style is not related to the self-expression emotional intelligence sub-scales.

Hypothesis 2a (alternative): Dismissive attachment style is related to the Self-Expression Emotional Intelligence subscale. Hypothesis 2b (null): Dismissive attachment style is not related to the Decision-Making emotional intelligence sub-scales. Hypothesis 2b (alternative): Dismissive attachment style is related to the Decision-Making Emotional Intelligence subscale. Hypothesis 2c (null): Dismissive attachment style is unrelated to the self-perception t emotional intelligence sub-scale. Hypothesis 2c (alternative): Dismissive attachment style is related to the Self-perception Emotional Intelligence subscale. Hypothesis 2d (null): Dismissive attachment style is not positively related to the stress management emotional intelligence sub-scales. Hypothesis 2d (alternative): Dismissive attachment style is positively related to the Stress-management Emotional Intelligence subscale. Hypothesis 2e (null): Dismissive attachment style is not positively related to the interpersonal emotional intelligence sub-scales. Hypothesis 2e (alternative): Dismissive attachment style is positively related to the interpersonal Emotional Intelligence subscale.

Research Question 3: Is there a significant correlation between fearful attachment style as measured by RSQ (Griffin & Batholomew, 1994) and emotional

intelligence subscales (Stress Management, Self -
Perception, Self-Expression, Interpersonal, and decision-
making) as measured by EQ2.0-I (Bar-On, 1997)?

Hypothesis 3a (null): The fearful attachment
style is not positively related to the stress
management emotional intelligence sub-scales.
Hypothesis 3a (alternative): Fearful attachment
style is positively related to the Stress
management Emotional Intelligence subscale.
Hypothesis 3b (null): Fearful attachment style
is not positively related to the decision-making
emotional intelligence sub-scales.
Hypothesis 3b (alternative): Fearful attachment
style positively affects related to the decision-
making emotional Intelligence subscale.
Hypothesis 3c (null): Fearful attachment style
is not positively related to the self-perception
emotional intelligence sub-scales.
Hypothesis 3c (alternative): Fearful attachment
style is positively related to the self-perception
Emotional Intelligence subscale.
Hypothesis 3d(null): Fearful attachment style is
not positively related to the interpersonal
emotional intelligence sub-scales.
Hypothesis 3d (alternative): Fearful attachment
style is positively related to the interpersonal
Emotional Intelligence subscale.
Hypothesis 3e(null): Fearful attachment style is
not positively related to the self-expression
emotional intelligence sub-scales.

Hypothesis 3e (alternative): Fearful attachment style is positively related to the self-expression Emotional Intelligence subscale.

Research Question 4: Is there a significant correlation between preoccupied attachment style as measured by RSQ (Griffin & Batholomew, 1994) and emotional intelligence subscales (Stress Management, Self-Perception, Self-Expression, Interpersonal, and decision-making) as measured by EQ2.0-I (Bar-On, 1997)?

Hypothesis 4a (null): Preoccupied attachment style is not positively related to the stress management emotional intelligence sub-scales.

Hypothesis 4a (alternative): Preoccupied attachment style is positively related to the Stress-management Emotional Intelligence subscale.

Hypothesis 4b (null): Preoccupied attachment style is not positively related to the Decision-Making emotional intelligence sub-scales.

Hypothesis 4b (alternative): Preoccupied attachment style is positively related to the Decision-Making Emotional Intelligence subscale.

Hypothesis 4c (null): Preoccupied attachment style is not positively related to the self-perception management emotional intelligence sub-scales.

Hypothesis 4c (alternative): Preoccupied attachment style is positively related to the self-perceptions Emotional Intelligence subscale.

Hypothesis 4d (null): Preoccupied attachment style is not positively related to the interpersonal emotional intelligence sub-scales. Hypothesis 4d (alternative): Preoccupied attachment style positively relates to the interpersonal Emotional Intelligence subscale. Hypothesis 4e (null): Preoccupied attachment style is not positively related to the self-expression emotional intelligence sub-scales. Hypothesis 4d (alternative): Preoccupied attachment style positively relates to the self-expression Emotional Intelligence subscale.

Research Question 5: Will the total score of attachment style as measured by RSQ (Griffin & Batholomew, 1994) predicts emotional intelligence as measured by EQI-2.0 (Bar-On, 1997) based on moderating effects of age, gender, and race?

Hypothesis 5 (null): Attachment style as measured by RSQ (Griffin & Batholomew, 1994) does not predict emotional intelligence as measured by EQI-2.0 (Bar-On, 1997) based on moderating effects of age, gender, or race.

Hypothesis 5 (alternative): Attachment style as measured by RSQ (Griffin & Batholomew, 1994) predicts emotional intelligence as measured by EQI-2.0 (Bar-On, 1997) based on moderating effects of age, gender, or race.

Hypothesis 5A (null): Attachment style as measured by RSQ (Griffin & Batholomew, 1994) does not predict emotional intelligence as measured by EQI-2.0 (Bar-On, 1997) based on moderating effects of age.

Hypothesis 5A (alternative): Attachment style, as measured by RSQ (Griffin & Batholomew, 1994), predicts emotional intelligence, as measured by EQI-2.0 (Bar-On, 1997), based on moderating effects of age.

Hypothesis 5B (null): Attachment style, as measured by RSQ (Griffin & Batholomew, 1994), does not predict emotional intelligence, as measured by EQI-2.0 (Bar-On, 1997), based on moderating effects of gender.

Hypothesis 5B (alternative): Attachment style as measured by RSQ (Griffin & Batholomew, 1994) predicts emotional intelligence as measured by EQI-2.0 (Bar-On, 1997) based on moderating effects of gender.

Hypothesis 5C (null): Attachment style, as measured by RSQ (Griffin & Batholomew, 1994), does not predict emotional intelligence, as measured by EQI-2.0 (Bar-On, 1997) based on moderating effects of race.

Hypothesis 5C (alternative): Attachment style, as measured by RSQ (Griffin & Batholomew, 1994), predicts emotional intelligence, as measured by EQI-2.0 (Bar-On, 1997), based on moderating effects of race.

Nature of the Study

This research adopts a quantitative survey approach to investigate the relationship between attachment styles and emotional intelligence among

United States students. Drawing inspiration from prior research, particularly the findings of Hamarta et al. (2009), the study aims to employ rigorous statistical methods to analyze and quantify the associations between attachment styles and emotional intelligence. Using a quantitative survey allows systematic data collection and analysis, enabling the exploration of patterns and trends measurably and objectively. By leveraging a survey-based methodology, the study seeks to provide numerical insights into the predictive nature of attachment styles on emotional intelligence, contributing to the growing body of empirical knowledge in this domain.

Significance of Study

The proportion of individuals who experience behavior problems due to poor emotional intelligence and poor attachment styles is relatively high. There is a need to determine whether there is a relationship between emotional intelligence subscales and attachment styles subscales, as the extent of this relationship will help determine the best method to correct or improve this in people. Therefore, there is a need to determine whether people who score high or low in emotional intelligence have a specific pattern of attachment style and vice versa. The current study will also determine whether age, gender, and race have moderating effects on emotional intelligence and attachment styles.

This study aims to investigate whether there is a significant relationship between emotional intelligence and attachment style in United States students, as determined by Hamarta et al. (2009) among Turkish students. The participants will complete several measures to obtain EI and attachment style. The current study will contribute to the knowledge of the practical use of emotional intelligence and attachment style in a different setting compared to previous findings in other settings; if outcomes are similar, then findings will be regarded as reliable, valid, and generalizable.

This study contributes to the field of psychology by helping us to understand the relationship between EI and attachment styles. It will also add to the current research about attachment styles predicting EI; thereby, correcting a person's attachment style may improve their emotional intelligence. Mental health workers could focus on enhancing the attachment styles of a person with emotional dysregulation and may be able to see an improvement in the person's emotional intelligence. The original study used Bar-on EQi, which has since become obsolete. The only version available is EQi 2.0.

Table 1

Definition of Terms

Emotional Intelligence 2.0 Subscale (Mayer et al., 2002a).

Interpersonal EI	Include interpersonal relationships, empathy, and social responsibility
Self-Perception EI	Includes self-regard, self-actualization, and emotional self-awareness.
Stress-Management EI	Include flexibility, stress- management, and optimism.
Decision-Making EI	Include problem-solving, reality testing, and impulse control
Self-Expression EI	Include emotional expression, assertiveness, and independence

Emotional Intelligence and Emotional Intelligence 1.0 Subscale by Oxford Dictionary, 2023

Emotional Intelligence (EI)	The ability to recognize, manage, and articulate one's emotions and navigate interpersonal connections with wisdom and empathy. Perceptiveness and skill in dealing with emotions and interpersonal relationships
Adaptability	The ability to conform to new environments and conditions.
Adaptation	The ability to conform to new environments and conditions; the action of adapting one thing to fit with another condition.
General good mood	A temporary state of mind or feeling.

Interpersonal | The abilities that enable effective communication and social interaction between people.

Intrapersonal | It occurs inside a person's mind or character. on the inside, within, affecting, or belonging to a particular person rather than anyone else.

Stress Management | The ability to process or control external and internal pressures.

Attachment Styles and attachment styles subscale (Ainsworth et al., 1978)

Attachment Styles (AS) | A manner of affection and behavioral system that promotes proximity to others and facilitates protection.

Secure AS | A manner of affection that is untroubled by fear or apprehension.

Dismissive AS or Avoidant | A manner of affection that avoids proximity and interaction with a partner, where the typical response would be to seek proximity

| Preoccupied AS or Ambivalent Anxious | A manner of affection that seeks a combination of resistance and seeking to gain and maintain contact |
| Fearful AS | A manner of affection that continually seeks proximity |

Assumption and Limitations

This study assumes that EI and attachment style measurements are theoretically valid and that the methods used to analyze each construct are valid and reliable. It also presumes that participants will provide truthful self-report data. The sample will be restricted to individuals willing and able to participate and those with access to the survey. Another potential limitation is the reliability of quantitative studies reliant on self-reporting, given the potential for participants to manipulate responses to produce more favorable outcomes. Additionally, the population sampled will be limited to students in the continental United States, thus restricting the generalizability of the results.

Expected Findings

The expected findings of this study suggest a predictive relationship between attachment styles and emotional intelligence using regression analyses (Hamarta et al., 2009). Specifically, the predicted finding is a significant correlation between EI subscales -- Stress Management, Self -Perception, Self-Expression, Interpersonal, and Decision-making -- and attachment style subscales, including secure, dismissive, preoccupied, and fearful attachment styles.

This research contributes to the mental health field, as correlations in emotional intelligence may relate positively to attachment styles. These expected findings aim to contribute valuable insights into the interconnected dynamics of emotional intelligence and attachment styles, offering potential avenues for targeted interventions to enhance psychological well-being and interpersonal relationships.

Chapter 2.

Literature Review

This chapter summarizes existing research on attachment styles and emotional intelligence (EI) and the gaps in the existing literature, which will support the need for this replication study of the predictive ability of attachment style and emotional intelligence. The information in this literature review will focus on attachment styles (secure, dismissive, fearful, and preoccupied attachment styles) and emotional intelligence (interpersonal, stress management, self-expression, and decision-making emotional intelligence). This discussion will demonstrate the relationship between attachment styles and emotional intelligence, suggesting that there may be a predictive relationship between emotional intelligence and attachment styles.

Theoretical Orientation of Emotional Intelligence

The concept of emotional intelligence and its precursors were relatively brief. It started in the 1920s when Edward Thorndike described social intelligence as the ability to get along with people. Later, David Weschler's 1939 theory of intelligence defined intelligence as definable only through behavior optimally adapted to the environment and not as a separate cognitive faculty (The Origin, 2020). The concept of Emotional strength, which is the ability to manage emotions effectively, was first introduced in the 1950s by Abraham Maslow; he was an American psychologist who created Maslow's Hierarchy of Needs, a psychological health theory on how humans fulfill their needs, by first fulfilling their basic needs before being able to address the more advanced needs (Maslow, 1954). The term emotional intelligence appeared in 1964 in Beldoch's research titled "Sensitivity to the expression of emotional meaning in three modes of Communication (Beldoch,1964), and in 1966 in Leuner's research titled "Emotional Intelligence and Emancipation" (Leuner, 1966). Gardner's article introduced emotional intelligence subscales, such as interpersonal and intrapersonal intelligence (Gardner, 1983). Other publications on emotional intelligence include Beasley (1987), Greenspan (1989), and Salovey and Mayer (1990).

Development of Emotional Intelligence Concepts and Definitions

In 1985, Israeli psychologist Reuven Bar-On developed a quantitative approach to creating Emotional Quotient (EQ) and Intellectual Quotient (IQ), comparing the two scores in his doctoral dissertation. Bar-On showed social and emotional competencies as the determinant of the effectiveness of individuals' understanding and expressing themselves and their interaction with others as they cope with daily challenges and demands. The Bar-on concepts included awareness of emotion, understanding and expressing feelings, understanding the feelings of others and the method of interaction, controlling and managing emotions, managing changes, solving problems of personal and interpersonal nature, and generating positive enhancement of self-motivation by facilitating socially and emotionally intelligent behavior (The Origin, 2020).

The Bar-On concepts of emotional intelligence included 15 factors: optimism, self-actualization, reality testing, social responsibility, problem-solving, interpersonal skills, stress tolerance, independence, assertiveness, impulse control, empathy, reality testing, emotional expression, self-regard, emotional self-awareness, and flexibility (Bar-On, 2006). Mayer and Salovey (1990) defined emotional intelligence as the ability to perceive emotions in others and the self correctly, use emotions to think well, accurately use emotional language, understand emotions, send the correct emotional signals, and manage emotions to attain goals.

Other Definitions and Functions of Emotional Intelligence

Emotional intelligence is the expression, regulation, management, and appraisal of emotion, which also includes using emotional information in acting and thinking to obtain positive results (Hamarta et al., 2009). Other definitions of emotional intelligence are the ability to think about emotions and expand thinking using emotion. These include interpreting emotions correctly, assisting thought with feelings, understanding emotional knowledge and emotion, and reflecting emotions, leading to intellectual and emotional growth (Mayer et al., 2004).

Emotional intelligence is a general construct that comprises a broad spectrum of abilities that influence the ability of a person to cope effectively (Bar-On et al.,

2000). The function of emotion is to communicate needs, priorities, and motives to others and the self. Other functions of emotions are orientation, engagement, shaping meaning, motivation, communicating with others, and eliciting responses (Johnson, 2019). Learning is emotional and conditioned by culture and social situations. Emotion is the information processing system for survival and an adaptive behavioral and physiological response to evolutionary situations (Johnson, 2019). Finally, *emotional intelligence* is the ability to use, perceive, understand, and regulate emotions, positively influencing people's psychological and positive influences in social adjustments (Khan & Kamal, 2023; Salguero et al., 2015).

Figure 1

Diagram of emotional intelligence, emotional intelligence subscales, and emotional intelligence subscales definition.

Factors Affecting Emotional Intelligence

An important factor affecting emotional intelligence is the absence of a parental figure, which causes emotional and intellectual deprivation, leading to psychological maladjustment and psychological problems like mood disorders, attachment difficulties, and emotional issues (Khan & Kamal, 2023). Psychological problems develop in adolescents who do not form emotional connections with others when the need for security is not satisfied, and they cannot recognize and understand their emotions and other people's emotions. Some people will experience rejection in interpersonal and intrapersonal relationships because of negative personality traits like aggression, hostility, emotional dysregulation, negative self-image, and suspiciousness. They have reduced emotional intelligence due to emotional dysfunction, which results in psychological dispositions like depression, stress, aggression, hostility, loneliness, negative self-esteem, unstable interpersonal relationships, and cutting themselves off from others (Khan & Kamal, 2023).

There is a significantly negative correlation between emotional intelligence, attachment styles, and psychological maladjustment (Khan & Kamal, 2023). Khan and Kamal, 2023, assert that orphans, or children deprived of necessary parental love, can experience maladaptive attachment styles and low emotional intelligence. Another factor that affects emotional intelligence is self-esteem, which influences one's perception and evaluation of self. Self-esteem is a mediator of childhood and adulthood attachment, and adults with secure attachment score higher on self-esteem and low on psychological distress (Shen et al., 2021). Parental attachment is only part of what determines peer attachment in the second decade of life: Healthy and empowering peer relationships also lead to positive outcomes (McGinley & Evans, 2020).

The Most Widely Studied Theoretical Constructs of Emotional Intelligence (EI)

Petrides and Furnham categorized emotional intelligence (EI) as ability and trait EI in 2000. Another popular method of EI measurement introduced by Ashkanasy and Daus in 2005 included stream one ability measures, stream two Self-report, and stream three mixed models. The mixed model is a mixture of personality and behavioral items used to measure traits, social skills, competencies, and personality (O'Connor et al., 2019).

Ability EI

These are tests that use questions/items like IQ tests. This test does not rely on self-reports but on solving problems related to the participants' emotion-related issues, with either correct or incorrect answers. For example, what emotion will a person feel before an interview? A) Happy b) Sad c) nervous d) all the above (O'Connor et al., 2019). Ability-based measures help to measure individuals' ability to understand how emotion works. Ability tests do not predict regular behavior and measured traits because they are of maximal ability. Ability-based measures are suitable for the measurement of job satisfaction and job performance and are not faked (O'Connor et al., 2019).

Trait EI

These measures use self-report to measure EI and its sub-dimensions (O'Connor et al., 2019). These are for measures that are self-reported, like the present research. People with high scores in the traits have high levels of self-efficacy about emotion-related behaviors and can regulate emotions in themselves and others (O'Connor et al., 2019). Trait EI measures typical behaviors and not maximal performances and gives a good prediction of regular behavior in different situations. Trait EI determines different work attitudes, such as organizational commitment, job performance, and commitment (O'Connor et al., 2019).

Mixed EI

This questionnaire includes traits, competencies, social skills, and other personality measures (O'Connor et al., 2019). Mixed EI is a good measure of multiple emotion-related outcomes like organizational commitment and job satisfaction. Mixed EI also helps to develop emotional competencies that improve professional success (O'Connor et al., 2019). Mixed EI, Ability EI, and Trait EI overlap; they are hierarchical and measure conceptual overlaps. The three concepts measure perceiving emotions in self and others, regulating emotion in self and others, and utilizing emotion strategically (O'Connor et al., 2019).

Differences between Multiple Intelligences: Emotional Intelligence (EQ), Intellectual Intelligent (IQ) and Personality type

Significant differences exist between multiple intelligences: emotional intelligence, intellectual intelligence, and personality. The concept of multiple intelligence disputes the fact that there is only one type of intelligence -- intellectual intelligence (IQ) -- which predicts a person's ability to succeed academically. However, intelligence is the biopsychological ability of a species to process information in a certain way (Gardner, 2013). IQ tests a person's logical or mathematical intelligence, linguistic, and sometimes spatial intelligence, predicting who will perform well in school in the 20th century. Gardner, 2013, revealed that there are other intelligences, which include musical intelligence, social (interpersonal) intelligence, intrapersonal intelligence (understanding of self), bodily-kinesthetic intelligence, naturalist intelligence (to be able to differentiate between nature), existential intelligence, considerable question intelligence, pedagogical intelligence (ability to convey knowledge or skills to another person).

Multiple intelligence means a person can be intelligent in several distinct and sometimes mutually exclusive areas. For example, a person with high emotional intelligence does not necessarily mean he has high spatial intelligence (Gardner, 2013). Styles and intelligence are different psychological constructs; style is how one approaches a range of materials. Hence, personality style is how a person approaches others or themselves, and attachment style is how one builds a connection with oneself and others. Intelligence refers to the computational power of the mental system. For example, a person with high linguistic capabilities can compute information involving language. Multiple intelligence tests MIDAS (Shearer, 2013) determine people's preferences and interests. The neurological support of numerous intelligences is that intelligence occurs in distinct parts of the brain; Figure 1 below shows the different parts of the brain involved in various types of intelligence.

Figure 2
Diagram showing different parts of the brain responsible for different types of intelligence.
(Gardner, 2013)

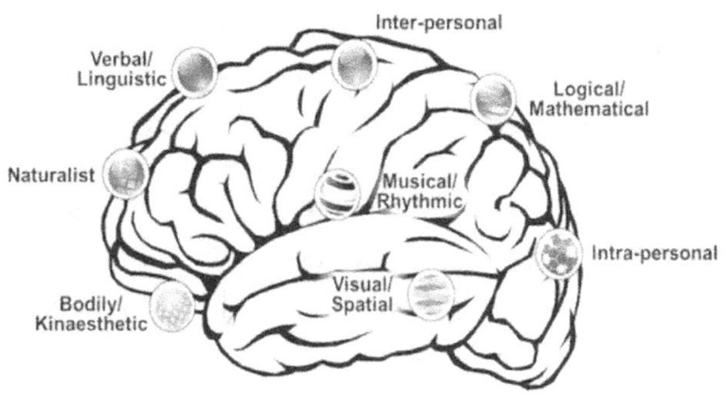

Multiple Intelligences
Howard Gardner: Frames of Mind

Emotional quotient (EQ) refers to the ability to feel, and intellectual quotient (IQ) refers to the ability to think, and high EQ means to be easily moved and express one's feelings (Beasley, 1987). A neural bridge was discovered between IQ and multiple intelligence as *intelligence* was defined as processing information in a biopsychological way that activates problem-solving in a cultural setting to create products (Gardner, 2000). Multiple intelligence is a product of nurture, not nature, which shows that general intelligence focusing on cognitive abilities is inaccurate. However, other intelligence, such as spiritual, moral, and existential, may not meet the criteria to be included (Gardner, 2011).

Emotional intelligence is a form of intelligence because it has the required four parts that make intelligence, which include emotional perception to be able to see emotions, emotional sensations such as reasoning, problem-solving, taste and color, emotional understanding that is solving emotional problems by identifying similar emotions, and emotional management understanding implications of social acts in self and others and regulating this social acts (Bar-On et al., 2000).

A test-to-test correlation of r=0.36 between a personality test and a self-report emotional intelligence test means the two tests have about 10 percent common variance. There were also correlations between emotional intelligence and empathy, parental warmth, life satisfaction measures, and broader aspects of personality (Bar-On et al., 2000).

Implications of Emotional Intelligence

Emotions arise in response to appraisals of different contexts, such as survival and reproduction. The abilities and skills associated with emotional intelligence are divided into perceived emotions, using emotion to facilitate thought, understanding emotions, and managing emotions (Mayer et al., 2004). Perceived emotion is measured by the recognition of people's facial expressions and asking people to compare emotions on people's faces to other things like landscapes, sensory stimuli, and emotions that will facilitate thinking and understanding; emotions are measured by testing a person's ability to determine the circumstances for emotional intensity, how emotional changes occur, and identifying emotions that arise in more complex situations (Mayer et al., 2004).

Managing emotions is measured through emotion management by asking about hypothetical situations, how the individual will change or maintain their emotion, and how to manage others' feelings to obtain the desired outcome (Mayer et al., 2004). People with high emotional intelligence can perceive emotions, use them in thought, understand their meanings, and manage their emotions (Mayer et al., 2004). Emotional symptoms and emotional intelligence are mainly relevant to the mediating effect of happiness; promoting emotional skills in emerging adults will promote good mental health and a happy mood, and people with high emotional skills can empathize more with others and experience more happiness (Ballester et al., 2022). In addition, teaching emotional regulation increases their perception and happiness capacity (Guerra-Bustamante et al., 2019). Intelligence, on the other hand, reveals that cognitive abilities increase with development, intelligence is relatively stable during development, cognitive skills covary over similar tests, there are different types of mental abilities or intelligence, and there is a universal type of cognitive ability in humans' beings that is not different from one another (Gardner et al., 1996).

Benefits and Qualities of Emotional Intelligence

Numerous studies showed that some benefits of emotional intelligence include higher job performance due to the ability to regulate emotions, leading to good relationships with others. An example of these benefits is when the US Air Force used EQ-1 to select new recruiters, and the most successful recruiters scored higher in emotional competencies of empathy, assertiveness, emotional self-awareness, and happiness (Cherniss, 1999). This method of selecting recruiters by the Air Force has increased the prediction of successful recruiters threefold, which brought about a gain of $3 million for the Air Force. Then, the method was adopted by all the other parts of the armed forces (Cherniss, 1999). Multinational consulting firms also assessed the emotional intelligence of their partners, and those that scored higher delivered over $1.2 million in profit from their accounts than other partners and had an increased gain of 139%. A study showed that three hundred top-level executives from fifteen global companies were tested on six emotional competencies, such as influence, self-confidence, team leadership, organizational awareness, leadership, and achievement drive, which were to distinguish the average leaders from the star leaders (Cherniss, 1999).

Further, L'Oreal sales agents who were selected based on emotional competencies outsold the sales representatives who were selected using the company's old method of selection by $91,370, a net revenue increase of $2,558,360 and a 63% less turnover (Cherniss, 1999).
National insurance company, sales agents with high emotional competencies sold policies worth $114,000, and those with low emotional competencies, sales agents in MetLife insurance that showed high optimism, sold 37 percent more life insurance, and how well people handle their emotions will determine how well people around them preferred to deal with them (Cherniss, 1999). A team leader's emotional intelligence positively impacts emotional competence and team performance, with emotionally competent group norms affecting team performance (Elizabeth &Wolff, 2008).

Other benefits include higher mental and physical well-being, another product of high emotional intelligence and higher self-efficacy (Omrod, 2012). An individual with high emotional intelligence will have self-awareness, which is the ability to understand and know oneself to make good life and business decisions (Johnson, 2019). Self-awareness will recognize his emotions and how they affect others, themselves, and their job performances. The qualities of emotional intelligence include self-awareness, self-regulation, empathy, and motivation (Omrod, 2012). A person who can self-regulate has impulse control, will be able to control errors made by them and their team, let go of mistakes, and will intelligently react, adapt, and embrace changes (Johnson, 2019). A person with empathy is aware and considers other people's feelings, gains people's trust, understands different cultures, and can quickly resolve and prevent conflict and misunderstanding (Johnson, 2019). Motivated people have passion for their goals, are intrinsically driven, persevere during challenging situations, and desire to learn with pride (Omrod, 2012). An emotionally intelligent person has humor, is approachable, listens actively, and communicates effectively (verbally and non-verbally) (Johnson, 2019).

Measuring Emotional Intelligence

The development of theoretical models of intelligence through tests to measure the concept began in the 1980s, with the development of EQ-I in 1983 (Bar-On et al., 2000). These measures aimed to identify factors related to practical social and emotional functioning and define them clearly, developing a psychometric measurement and generalization of the instrument across cultures (Bar-On et al., 2000). Emotional intelligence scales have been commonly used in EI measures of perceiving, regulating, and utilizing emotions (O'Connor et al., 2019). These EI measures are questionnaires that are usually self-reports. Below are standard scales used to measure EI.

      • Mayer-Salovey-Caruso Emotional Intelligence Tests (MSCEIT) (Mayer et al., 2002a) measure emotional perception (Identifying in the faces, in stories, in designs, and in music emotions), facilitation (translating feelings and making a judgment with emotions), understanding (defining emotions, complex emotional blends, transitions and perspectives), and management (managing others and self-emotion) (Bar-On et at.,2000)

      • Self-report Emotional Intelligence Test (SREIT) (Schutte et al., 1998)

      • Trait Emotional Intelligence Questionnaire (TEIQue) (Petrides and Furnham, 2001)

      • Bar-On Emotional Quotient Inventory (EQi) (Bar-On, 1997a: Bar-On, 1997b) measures intrapersonal (emotional self-awareness, self-regard, assertiveness, actualization, and independence), interpersonal (empathy, social responsibility, and interpersonal relationship), stress management (problem-solving, flexibility, and reality testing), adaptability (impulse control and stress tolerance), and general good mood (optimism and happiness) (Bar-On et al, 2000).

• The Situational Test of Emotional
Management (STEM) (MacCann & Roberts,
2008)
• The Situational Test of Emotional
Understanding (STEU) (MacCann & Roberts,
2008)
• The Emotional and Social Competence
Inventory (ESCI) (Boyatzis & Goleman, 2007)
measures self-awareness (emotional self-
awareness, self-confidence, and accurate self-
assessment), social awareness (empathy,
organizational awareness, and service-oriented),
self-management (self-control, trustworthiness,
conscientiousness, initiative, adaptability, and
achievement), and social skills (Developing
others, leadership, building bonds, catalyst
change, influence, conflict management,
teamwork, and communication. (Bar-On et al.,
2000).
• EQ-Map (Cooper, 1996/1997) measures the
current environment (life pressures, life
satisfaction), emotional literacy (emotional self-
awareness, expression, awareness of others), EQ
competencies (intentionality, creativity,
resilience, interpersonal connections,
constructive discontent)) EQ values and attitude
(compassion, outlook, personal power,
integrated self, and trust radius) EQ outcomes (
General health, quality of life, optimal
performance, and relationship quotient (Bar-On
et al., 2000).

Emotional Intelligence Theoretical Construct Used for the Present Study.

The consideration of the measure used to evaluate the EQ is the aspect of mental life to be measured based on its content validity (that is, the test measuring what the test claims to measure) (Bar-On et al., 2000). The EQ-I used in Hamarta et al., 2009, is an older version of the EQ-2.0 used in this study. The EQ-I resulted from 20 years of Dr. Reuven Bar-On's work, which consists of 133 items for the five emotional intelligence subscales included in this study. While the EQ-I and EQ-2.0 are similar, the main difference is that EQ-2.0 allows adding the multi-rater EQ 360 (The Myers-Briggs, 2023). The EQ 360 multi-rater assessment combines the self-reported EQ with the perceptions of others who know the participant well.

The EQ 360 is not required in this study, EQ-I 2.0 will be used because it is like EQ-I, and EQ-I 2.0 is the version available for the present study. The test for the present study measures diverse types of non-cognitive capabilities, skills, and competencies that affect a person's ability to successfully navigate environmental pressures and demands (Bar-On et al., 2000). The mixed resent study will use mixed EQ because the mixed method uses the participants' abilities and personalities to evaluate their emotional intelligence. The EQ-2.0 (Bar-On) measures a mixed model of EQ.

Attachment Style Theory

In 1958, Bowlby identified five behaviors - smiling, clinging, following, crying, and sucking, that create an attachment between the mother and child, which will later develop into attachment behavior that is sensitive to environmental context and cues (Bowlby, 1958). The secure base behavior at home approach removes the psychoanalysis aspects of attachment theory. It introduces the motivational approach that explains the child's sensitivity to the environment and the child going back and forth to his mother (Ainsworth et al.,1978). The nature of infant-mother relationships in normative (personal and interpersonal processes that make one behave in a socially acceptable way) and evolutionary perspectives (personality and individual differences based on adaptive survival and reproduction) focused on the behavior patterns of infants' interest in the physical and social environment. These normative patterns explain the issue with psychoanalytic theory (why people behave when they behave) and operant conditioning (use of rewards and punishments to change behaviors) in explaining attachment theory (Ainsworth et al.,1978).

The field of psychology understood and accepted attachment theory because of a solid normative concept of attachment-exploration balance in different scenarios (Ainsworth et al.,1978). John Bowlby refers to attachment theory as a new paradigm of understanding the connection between mother and child. The attachment paradigm refers to the collaboration between Bowlby and Ainsworth and the community that shared and contributed to the attachment theory (Ainsworth et al.,1978). The secure base phenomenon is that most mammals can seek proximity contact at an early age, which supports exploration and learning. The book *Patterns of Attachment*, first published in 1978 by

Ainsworth, gave an in-depth explanation of attachment theory and the research on the strange situation procedure that led to these findings. The strange situation procedure (SSP) evolves from describing children's separation from their parents to testing the secure base phenomenon and the attachment-exploration balance.

The strange situation involves the participants, an infant, and his mother, in a room introduced to eight episodes in a particular order, with the least stressful episode occurring first. They observed that the infant would leave the mother's side to explore the toys strategically placed around the room (Ainsworth et al., 1978). Then, the child was left alone in the room, and a stranger entered the room. The physical environment, such as the diverse types of rugs, cabinets, and locations, was manipulated during the study. The stranger interacts with the mother and the baby, the mother leaves the room, and the stranger stops interacting with the child and sits quietly. The experimenters timed and recorded the baby's reaction, which the participants could not see. The expected reactions from the child include searching for the mother, crying, and playing with toys. The outcome of the strange situation study was conspicuous avoidance, where the baby ignores his mother on her return or casually acknowledges her. The second outcome is the baby wanting contact or proximity with the mother. The third outcome is the child displaying conspicuous contact and interaction-resisting behavior that may be maladaptive.

Why Study Attachment Styles Theory

Attachment theory shows that parents' response to children's emotional difficulties constructs the child's ability to empathize with other people (Stefan et al., 2019). Attachment theory is an interpersonal theory that puts people in the context of their closest relationships; hence, people are social and bond with others, which is an intrinsic survival strategy (Johnson, 2019). Children with secure attachments can empathize better with peers in distress than those with insecure attachments (Stefan et al., 2019). Attachment quality will affect children's social-emotional development. The attachment relationship is how a child bonds with his caregiver based on the caregiver's response to the child's needs (Stefan et al., 2019

Impact of Attachment Style on Relationship with Caregivers

Longitudinal research shows that secure attachment for two years, effective sharing of toys, and empathy to strangers demonstrate an understanding of others' thoughts and feelings at age four compared to avoidant and ambivalently attached children (Ştefan & Avram, 2019). Attachment developments are usually consistent from childhood to adulthood. Dismissive parenting affects a child's ability to deal with other people's emotions; children with secure attachment styles perform better than avoidantly attached children in empathic perspective-taking, and securely attached children compared to ambivalently attached children will perform higher in behavioral perspective-taking (Ștefan & Avram, 2019).

Based on longitudinal findings, friendship quality in early adulthood is best predicted by alienation from the parents, showing the development of socio-emotional and gender differences from adolescence to early adulthood (Zvara et al., 2020). Parent attachment is a continuous adaptive function from childhood to adulthood, and parent and peer attachment enhance emotional competencies such as positive expressiveness and emotional awareness that produce prosocial behaviors. Household chaos and insecure attachment styles are related to poor parenting behavior quality (Zvara et al., 2020). The stress of a highly disorganized family causes the mother to be insecure, more intrusive, and less sensitive parenting behavior, which leads to insecure attachment to the child.

Effect of Negative Attachment Style

Adult attachment styles may cause mental health problems, with anxious and avoidant attachments linked directly to mental illness, and there is the possibility of psychological risk with avoidant attachments, which positively causes mental health problems (Wei-Wen et al., 2022). People with secure attachments have the assurance that their partners will be available for them when needed, and insecure attachments include avoidant and anxious attachments. People with anxious attachments are frustrated when the need for attachment is unmet and worry about abandonment and rejection. In contrast, people with avoidant attachments are uncomfortable with intimacy and closeness. Rejection by the primary caregiver causes insecure attachment, which causes depression and distress.

There was a negative correlation between self-esteem and anxious and avoidant adult attachment. There is a positive correlation between anxious attachment and mental health problems and a negative correlation between mental health problems and anxious attachment (Wei-Wen et al., 2022). Self-esteem partially mediates the relationship between anxious and avoidant adult attachment and mental health problems, and avoidant and anxious attachments are related to low self-esteem. Self-esteem increases with positive relationships, which increases self-esteem and helps maintain good mental health. Adults with secure attachment scores lower in psychological distress and higher in self-esteem, and self-esteem are a significant mediator in attachment style for children and adults and influence how one sees and evaluates oneself (Shen et al., 2021).

The article focused on the mediating effect of self-esteem in mental health problems and adult attachment and suggested that self-esteem problems are some mental health problems caused by adult attachment styles (Wei-Wen, 2022 There is a negative correlation between avoidant attachments and mental health problems and anxious attachments to mental health problems. Psychological risk and mental health problems are growing risk factors. People with secure attachments have the assurance of their partner's support. People with insecure attachments are avoidant or dismissing and anxious or preoccupied attachment styles (Wei-Wen, 2022). Due to unmet attachment needs, a person with anxious attachments becomes chronically worried about abandonment and rejection and becomes frustrated. In avoidant or dismissive attachment styles, individuals are distant from people close to them and uncomfortable with intimacy and interpersonal closeness (Wei-Wen, 2022).

Insecure attachments (dismissive, preoccupied, and fearful) are because of rejection from the primary caregiver and are linked to depression and mental distress. Self-esteem is positively correlated with anxious and avoidant attachment, and anxious attachment is positively correlated with mental health problems (Wei-Wen, 2022). Anxious, avoidant attachment and mental health problems are mediated partially by self-esteem, and self-esteem is positively related to mental health problems (r=-.28, p<.001) (Wei-Wen, 2022). Moreover, avoidant and anxious attachments are both related to low self-esteem. Self-esteem plays a vital role in mental health problems, and positive relationships with partners increase self-esteem and positive motivation to maintain good mental health.

Internalizing symptomatology is problems experienced by individuals like loneliness, sadness, and anxiety and can be predicted through maternal and peer attachment; maternal attachment predicts peer attachment outcomes, but paternal attachment does not (McGinley & Evans, 2020). Young adults in their 20s and 30s with secure attachments to caregivers and peers usually have high coping skills, prosocial behavior, self-esteem, and emotional regulation (McGinley & Evans, 2020). The relationship with peers, maternal and paternal, is positively intercorrelated but positively correlated with depression, stress, and anxiety, while emotional, dire, complaint altruistic prosocial behaviors are positively correlated with peer attachment (McGinley & Evans, 2020). Depression, anxiety, and stress are directly and positively related to maternal and peer attachment and positively related to emotional prosocial behaviors (McGinley & Evans, 2020). Emotional and prosocial behavior are positively linked to internalizing symptomatology and individual differences in multiple socializing agents to attachment relationships into adulthood, which are critical for socioemotional adjustment (McGinley & Evans, (2020).).

The Four Types of Attachment Styles

Attachment is the emotional bond that provides safety, comfort, and support to another person. Parents and children have affection bonds when they have attachment behaviors. On the other hand, attachment theory explains attachment as mental models developed with others from infancy to adulthood, which organize and unify individual experiences and beliefs and include other people's characteristics. Positive and negative perceptions of self and others divide attachment style into secure, dismissing, preoccupied, and fearful (Hamarta et al., 2009). Secure attachment means that the individual can cope with negative emotions and have positive feelings for self and others. Therefore, the individual with secure attachment has positive emotions, positive emotional regulation skills, perception, understanding, facilitation, and management of emotions (Hamarta et al., 2009).

The secure attachment style can be traced to a sensitive and loving caregiver with an organized strategy for dealing with distress (Benoit, 2004). Dismissing attachment style involves negative feelings about others and positive thinking about self; sometimes referred to as insecure avoidants may have experienced insensitive and rejecting caregivers, with an organized strategy for dealing with stress (Benoit, 2004). The preoccupied attachment style, also called anxious-ambivalent, is when one has positive feelings about others and negative/anxiety about oneself. Also referred to as insecure-resistant, they may have had insensitive and inconsistent caregivers with organized methods of dealing with stress (Benoit, 2004). An individual with a fearful attachment style, the individual has negative feelings about others and negative feelings about self. Also referred to as an insecure-disorganized style, it may have had an atypical caregiver with a disorganized method of dealing with distress (Benoit, 2004). Attachment theory is the emotional-regulation model, where the internal working model regulates a person's emotional reaction to stressful situations, regulates emotions, and orients behaviors, as shown in Table 2.

Table 2

Showing attachment theory, features, and types

Attachment Style	Thought about Self	Thought about Partner	Features
Secure	Positive	Positive	Mutual trust and support, Healthy boundaries, Positive emotions, positive emotional regulation skills, perception, understanding, facilitation, and management of emotions.
Dismissive (also referred to as avoidant attachment)	Positive	Negative	Avoid intimacy, avoid vulnerability, be emotionally distant, and downplay the importance of relationships, insecure self-reliance, and independence.
Preoccupied (also referred to as anxious/ambivalent attachment)	**Negative**	Positive	Fear of abandonment needs validation dependence on a partner, insecure and poor communication.

Fearful (also referred to as disorganized attachment)	Negative	Negative	Fear of rejection, lack of trust, low self-esteem, and relationship anxiety.

Characteristics and Quality of the Four Types of Attachment Styles

The characteristics and qualities of the four major attachment styles, including secure, dismissive, preoccupied, and fearful, affect individuals' social-emotional development. The attachment relationship is how a child bonds with his caregiver based on the caregiver's response to the child's needs (Stefan & Avram, 2019). Attachment theory focuses on emotion, emotion regulation, secure base, cognitive perspective-taking, behavioral perspective-taking, affective perspective-taking, and fear. Fear is anxiety, helplessness, and vulnerability, which indicate survival concerns regarding death, isolation, loneliness, and loss, and dealing with them to increase resilience, vitality, growth, and flexible adaptiveness (Johnson, 2019). A secure base depends on the ability to rely on a loved one, which provides the base for moving into the world, exploring, taking risks, and developing a sense of autonomy and competencies (Johnson, 2019).

Cognitive perspective-taking is understanding the other person's perspective and the causes of their emotions. In comparison, behavioral perspective-taking uses prosocial behavior to respond to others' negative emotions (Stefan & Avram, 2019). Children at the age of four were in two years of longitudinal research on the effective sharing of toys and empathy with strangers; it showed that children with secure attachment were more empathetic and shared toys more than kids with avoidant and ambivalent attachment styles. Although attachment developments are usually consistent from childhood to adulthood, deficiency will lead to mental health problems (Stefan & Avram, 2019). Affective perspective-taking matches one emotion and others' emotional experiences. Affective perspective-taking has neural circuitry similar to that of emotion regulation.

The secure connection is the primary bonding relationship between people's patterns of encoding methods of interaction methods into mental models or methods of responding (Johnson, 2019). Therefore, attachment security changes with new experiences that change the cognitive working models of attachment and emotional regulation strategies (Johnson, 2019). Individuals with secure attachments are comfortable with closeness and need for other people. Attachment security calms the nervous system when a response is received, which buffers stress and provides coping skills throughout life (Johnson, 2019). Another model or strategy is when others are perceived as inaccessible or unresponsive (Johnson, 2019). The bonds between adults are more reciprocal and not dependent on proximity, such as child-parent attachment.

Security can be associated with intimacy, pleasure, and a higher level of arousal (Johnson, 2019).

Securely attached people are said to develop an internal working model on how to respond to the distress of others based on the response they received for their distress (Stefan & Avram, 2019). People with secure attachment styles perform better than avoidantly attached people in empathic perspective-taking. Also, the study confirmed that securely attached people, compared to ambivalently attached people, will perform higher on behavioral perspective-taking (Stefan & Avram, 2019).

Furthermore, People with avoidant attachment were associated with dismissive caregivers of emotional distress and paid little or no attention to the distress of their peers. Ambivalently attached people have inconsistent parenting responses to their negative emotions and are more preoccupied and anxious over their own negative emotions than considering their peer's negative emotions. People with disorganized attachment styles are exposed to frightening or alarming caregivers, limiting their abilities to manifest empathy (Stefan & Avram, 2019). At the same time, dismissive parenting affects a child's ability to attend to other people's emotions. The main factors of quality and security attachment bond are comprehended accessibility, responsiveness, and emotional engagement (A.R.E.) to attachment figure (are people there for me?) (Johnson, 2019). Separation of distress arises when a secure connection is lost, or an attachment bond threat (Johnson, 2019).

Measuring Attachment Styles

Attachment styles use measurement questionnaire instruments, such as self-report surveys. The adult attachment scale (TAS) (Collins & Read, 1990) is a self-reported measurement scale for attachment. Participants chose a scale of 1 to 5, where one was not characteristic of self, and five was very characteristic of self, answering questions like "I find it relatively easy to get close to others." The TAS has three subscales: Depend, Close, and Anxiety. The Close scale measures how much a person can depend on others for intimacy and closeness. The Depend scale measures how much a person can rely on others to be available when needed. The anxiety subscale measures how much a person worries about being unloved or abandoned. The scale can also measure two subscales of Avoidance and anxiety. The revised adult attachment scale (Collins, 1996) is like the adult attachment scale but with a few alterations to the questions and the scoring. The AAS and RAAS both contain three dimensions: discomfort with dependency, discomfort with closeness, and anxiety.

Close relationships-relationship structures (ECR-RS) questionnaire (Marszal, 2014) is another instrument used to measure attachment styles, and ECR-RS assesses avoidant and anxious attachment in interpersonal relationships. It uses a Likert scale of 1 to 7, where 1 strongly disagrees, and seven strongly agree. The revised Adult Attachment Scale (RAAS) (Collins, 1996) is an 18-item measure of an individual's intimacy and comfort (Collins, 1996). The adult attachment questionnaire (Simpson et al., 1996) has relationship questions with a 6-point Likert scale of 1 to 7, where 1 strongly disagrees and 7 strongly agrees. This instrument classifies attachment patterns in only two dimensions: avoidant attachment and anxiety attachment.

Relationship Between cognitive schemas, attachment style and emotional intelligence

Cognitive Schema is the mental framework of one's knowledge; assumptions about the world are the broad organizing principle used to interpret added information about oneself and the environment and to solve problems (Scarlat, 2021). A relationship exists between cognitive schemas, attachment style, and emotional intelligence. Cognitive schemas follow a person's life, which is composed of negative thoughts that cannot easily be changed, just like attachment style and emotional intelligence. Cognitive schemas influence attachment style by increasing or reducing it, and emotional intelligence is affected by cognitive patterns and deep-rooted beliefs. Cognitive schemas affect the relationship between attachment styles and emotional intelligence; cognitive schema also mediates the relationship between attachment styles and emotional intelligence (Scarlat, 2021).

Attachment Style Theoretical Construct Used for the Present Study

The present study will use the relationship scale questionnaire (RSQ) (Grifin & Bartholomew, 1994). The RSQ contains 17 items on attachment patterns and may include 13 items from other researchers. The RSQ has four subscales: Secure attachment, anxious attachment, avoidant attachment, and disorganized attachment.

Studies Examining the Relationship Between Attachment Styles and Emotional Intelligence

This research examines the relationship between Attachment style (IV) and emotional intelligence (DV): emotional intelligence (EQ) subscale: self-awareness, self-management, empathy, social awareness, and social skills. Self-management includes self-awareness and self-management. Self-awareness includes empathy, social awareness, and social skills. Self-awareness includes internal state preferences, resources, and intuition (Hamarta et al., 2009).

Secure attachment is positively related to all the subscales of emotional intelligence; there is a positive relationship between secure attachment style to interpersonal, intrapersonal, adaptability, stress management, and general good mood emotional intelligence. Dismissive attachment style was negatively related to interpersonal and intrapersonal emotional intelligence and positively associated with adaptive, Stress management, and general good health emotional intelligence. Fearful attachment style was negatively associated with all the emotional intelligence subscales;

hence, fearful attachment style will have the lowest emotional intelligence score. Preoccupied attachment style is only positively related to interpersonal emotional intelligence and negatively associated with intrapersonal, adaptability, and stress management emotional intelligence.

Figure 3

The diagram shows the results of Hamarta et al.'s research (2009), with black lines showing positive relationships and red lines showing negative relationships.

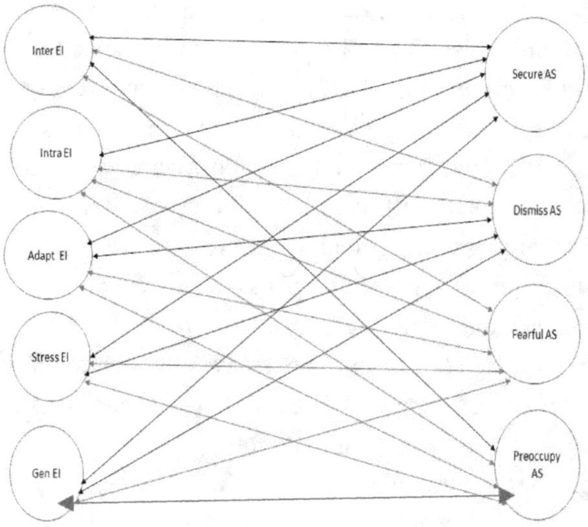

Table 3

Attachment theory and emotional intelligence: Summary of Working Definitions by Hamarta et al., 2009.

Self-Management	Managing a person's internal state and impulses facilitates reaching one's goals.
Social Awareness	Awareness of others' needs, concerns, and feelings
Empathy	The essential skill in relationships with others
Social Skills	The ability to get the correct response from other people, including communication, leadership, change catalyst, building bonds, teamwork, competencies of leadership, development of others, and collaboration
Emotional Intelligence	Interpersonal relationships, life satisfaction, and work-life determine the quality of emotional intelligence.

social and emotional competencies skills	Emotional-social intelligence shows how well one expresses and understands oneself and others, communicates, and copes with daily demands. It includes intrapersonal intelligence, interpersonal intelligence, adaptability, stress management, and general mood emotional intelligence subdimensions.
Intrapersonal EQ	Assertiveness, independence, self-actualization, emotional self-awareness, self-regard, knowing their emotions, and can easily express emotions and thoughts, and control themselves
Interpersonal emotional intelligence	Includes interpersonal relationships, empathy, and social responsibility as understanding how others feel, getting along, and communicating well with them
Adaptability EQ	Includes reality testing, problem-solving, and flexibility
Stress Management EQ	One can control impulses, stress, and cold-blooded
General Mood EQ	Includes hopefulness and confidence about the future and happiness

Attachment To be an affectionate and intimate relationship between two people, showing affection or fondness to another person, such as a parent or child, which provides safety, comfort, and support.

Attachment style theory Describe attachment as mental models developed by people with others in infancy, childhood, and adulthood. This mental model organizes and unifies individual experiences and beliefs and includes other people's characteristics. Attachment is the internal working model regulating a person's emotional reaction to stressful situations, where emotions are regulated, and behaviors are oriented.

Secure attachment involves positive feelings of self and others, the ability to cope with negative emotions in social interactions, and the possession of positive emotions.

Emotional regulation of skills and involvement in perceiving, understanding, facilitating, and managing emotions.

Dismissing or avoidant attachment style Shows positive feelings about self and negative feelings about others.

The preoccupied or an anxious ambivalent attachment style	Shows anxiety about self and positive feelings about others
Fearful attachment style	Shows negative feelings about both self and others

Justifying the Gap Between Attachment Styles and Emotional Intelligence Studies

Before the study by Hamarta et al. (2009), most studies focused on either attachment style or Emotional intelligence, not both (Hamarta et al., 2009). Other studies on attachment styles showed the advantage of attachment style that securely attached children compared to ambivalently attached children will perform higher on behavioral perspective-taking suggested future studies focus on identifying potential moderate effects of children's behavioral inhibition on empathic perspective-taking and a replication of the study in a laboratory or clinical setting (Ştefan et al., J. (2019). However, the study had limitations of low representation of children from low socio-economic status, the limited verbal ability of the children, and the need for longitudinal designs (Ştefan & Avram, 2019).

Secure attachment styles positively correlate with emotional intelligence (Hamarta et al, 2009). However, alcohol use disorders, depression, anxiety, stress, and decreased emotional intelligence are more common among people with preoccupied attachment styles (Obeid et al., 2019). Subjective well-being is influenced by self-esteem and emotional intelligence, which is predicted by a secure attachment style (Mittal & Rani, 2022). Additionally, secure attachment is a predictor of various parts of emotional intelligence, which means that attachment styles will explain emotional intelligence (Doktorová et al., 2020).

Furthermore, emotional intelligence is a mediating factor in the relationship between decision-making processes and secure attachment, which shows the mediating role of attachment style, emotional intelligence, and other psychological constructs (Phang et al., 2020). The study of Borawski et al. (2022) examined emotional intelligence as the mediator between loneliness and attachment styles in two cross-sectional studies, with 246 participants in the first study and 186 participants in the second study, which examined the mediating effect between loneliness, attachment style, and emotional intelligence. The study revealed that emotional intelligence mediates loneliness and attachment style, which means there is a connection between emotional intelligence and attachment style, even though that was not the primary focus of the research.

The research of Fabella et al. (2023) on the effect of the COVID-19 pandemic on attachment style and emotional intelligence used a sample size of 106 student volunteers and measured attachment style with the revised adult attachment scale (RAAS) and emotional intelligence with Schutte Self Report Emotional Intelligence. There was a positive relationship between emotional intelligence and close attachment style. The result of this study did not show the predictability of the emotional intelligence subscales and the attachment styles subscales. However, it showed a relationship between emotional intelligence and attachment styles.

Another study on attachment style and emotional intelligence by Yahya et al. (2019) examined adult attachment and emotional intelligence among University of Malaysia trainee counselors. The research identifies attachment style and emotional intelligence among 50 trainee counselors. The instrument used in Yahya et al.'s 2019 study experiences a close relationship (ECR) (Branner & Shaver, 2019), and Paul Michael developed an emotional intelligence self-assessment. The study suggests that people with attachment avoidance will have low emotional awareness. The study was based in a foreign country, Malaysia, and focused on one aspect of attachment style-avoidant attachment.

Current Study

Prior research indicates a relationship between attachment styles and emotional intelligence. Secure attachment styles are consistently associated with emotional intelligence and can forecast psychological outcomes, such as self-esteem and subjective well-being. Emotional intelligence also mediates the relationship between attachment styles and different aspects of psychological functioning, underscoring the significance of comprehending these constructs together.

The current study aims to replicate the Hamarta et al. (2009) study with an American sample using the updated (and currently available) version of the EQi. The

United States differs culturally, socially, and economically from Turkey; therefore, the present study may yield a different outcome. The Republic of Turkey attained independence in 1923 and changed its social and political views from those it inherited from the Ottoman Empire (Imamoglu, 2022). Islamic laws and principles govern Turkish people and speak the Turkish language in developing countries (Kocoglu, 2014). Additionally, developing countries bear a higher risk of pollution, which poses social and economic burdens due to environmental inequality (Shao et al., 2022). Therefore, students' standard of living in Turkey is relatively different from that of U.S. students. Hence, students in the United States may have other emotional Intelligence and attachment styles.

Chapter 3

Methodology

It includes study questions, design, hypotheses, data collection, measures, procedures, types of data analyses, expected findings, and ethical considerations.

Purpose of the Study

This study aims to replicate and generalize the findings of Hamarta et al. (2009) using a different approach in the United States. Generalization examines whether the original study's results hold across different settings, populations, treatments, or time, which will determine the validity of the original study when applied to a different population (Lund, 2012). Furthermore, this study seeks to validate and assess the generalizability of the research findings to the context of the United States, given that the original research was undertaken in Turkey fourteen years ago.

The study is a theory-driven dissertation focusing on the relationship between emotional intelligence and attachment styles. Its goal is to contribute theoretically to understanding how emotional intelligence predicts attachment styles and vice versa. Through this research, we aim to confirm the reliability and generalizability of previous findings in the field, particularly across diverse populations and educational settings (Handley et al., 2018).

The research aims to determine whether attachment styles will predict emotional intelligence within the U.S.

population, considering cultural and economic differences, as asserted in the research study by Hamarta (2009). This study examined the relationship between the four subscales of attachment styles (secure, dismissing, preoccupied, and fearful) and the five subscales of emotional intelligence (Stress Management, Self-perception, Self-Expression, Interpersonal, and Decision-Making). However, it is worth noting that the study of Hamarta (2009) utilized the emotional intelligence subscales of interpersonal, intrapersonal, stress management, adaptability, and general good mood, constituting the emotional intelligence version 1 instrument employed in their research. In contrast, the current study employs version 2 of the emotional intelligence EQ-2.0, comprising Stress Management, Self-perception, Self-Expression, Interpersonal, and Decision-Making subscales.

Research has shown that people with secure attachment have high emotional intelligence (Hamarta et al., 2009). This study intends to verify this assumption that secure attachment style predicts high emotional intelligence and determines the relationship between other attachment style subscales and emotional intelligence subscales. Attachment styles are practical and centered on individuals' feelings. Attachment style can be categorized into two categories, secure and insecure, while insecure attachment style includes the other three subscales: dismissive, disorganized, and fearful attachment styles. Individuals develop insecure attachment styles to protect themself from experiences of pain and anxiety (West et al., 1994). These goals on the survival instincts of humans linked to one another, and the termination of one system serves as the activation of another system (West et al.,1994). In other words, the termination of an insecure attachment style should produce a secure one, thereby increasing the individuals' emotional intelligence.

Another goal of the present study is to determine whether the total score of attachment style as measured by RSQ (Griffin & Batholomew, 1994) predicts emotional intelligence as measured by EQI-2.0 (Bar-On, 1997) based on the moderating effects of age, gender, and race. These will allow a better understanding of nature versus nurture effect on attachment style and emotional intelligence and determine whether environmental or genetic factors contribute to one's emotional intelligence and attachment style.

Moreover, the current study's findings will be significant as a comparative baseline for emotional intelligence and attachment styles for future research using these two constructs for a United States-based population. The study will also help us understand the need to promote emotional skills in emerging adults, leading to good mental health and happiness. However, understanding emotional intelligence and its relationship to attachment styles will provide a good base for intervention.

Research Questions and Hypotheses

Research Question 1: Is there a significant positive correlation between secure attachment style as measured by RSQ (Griffin & Batholomew, 1994) and emotional intelligence (Stress Management, Self-Perception, Self-

Expression, Interpersonal, and decision-making) as measured by EQ2.0-I (Bar-On, 1997)?

Hypothesis 1a (null): Secure attachment style is not positively related to the self-perception subscale of emotional intelligence.

Hypothesis 1a (alternative): Secure attachment style is positively related to the self-perception subscales of emotional intelligence.

Hypothesis 1b (null): Secure attachment style is not positively related to the self-expression subscale of emotional intelligence.

Hypothesis 1b (alternative): Secure attachment style is positively related to the self-expression subscales of emotional intelligence.

Hypothesis 1c (null): Secure attachment style is not positively related to the interpersonal subscale of emotional intelligence.

Hypothesis 1c (alternative): Secure attachment style is positively related to the interpersonal subscales of emotional intelligence.

Hypothesis 1d (null): Secure attachment style is not positively related to the decision-making subscale of emotional intelligence.

Hypothesis 1d (alternative): Secure attachment style is positively related to the Decision-Making subscales of emotional intelligence.

Hypothesis 1e (null): Secure attachment style is not positively related to the stress management subscale of emotional intelligence.

Hypothesis 1e (alternative): Secure attachment style is positively related to emotional intelligence stress management subscales.

Research Question 2: Is there a significant correlation between Dismissive attachment style as measured by RSQ (Griffin & Batholomew, 1994) and emotional intelligence subscales (Stress Management, Self - Perception, Self-Expression, Interpersonal, and decision-making) as measured by EQ2.0-I (Bar-On, 1997)?

Hypothesis 2a (null): Dismissive attachment style is unrelated to the self-expression emotional intelligence sub-scales.

Hypothesis 2a (alternative): Dismissive attachment style is related to the Self-Expression Emotional Intelligence subscale.

Hypothesis 2b (null): Dismissive attachment style is unrelated to the Decision-Making emotional intelligence sub-scale.

Hypothesis 2b (alternative): Dismissive attachment style is related to the Decision-Making Emotional Intelligence subscale.

Hypothesis 2c (null): Dismissive attachment style is unrelated to the self-perception t emotional intelligence sub-scale.

Hypothesis 2c (alternative): Dismissive attachment style is related to the Self-perception Emotional Intelligence subscale.

Hypothesis 2d (null): Dismissive attachment style is not positively related to stress management emotional intelligence sub-scales.

Hypothesis 2d (alternative): Dismissive attachment style is positively related to the

Stress-management Emotional Intelligence subscale.

Hypothesis 2e (null): Dismissive attachment style is not positively related to the interpersonal emotional intelligence sub-scales.

Hypothesis 2e (alternative): Dismissive attachment style is positively related to the interpersonal Emotional Intelligence subscale.

Research Question 3: Is there a significant correlation between fearful attachment style as measured by RSQ (Griffin & Batholomew, 1994) and emotional intelligence subscales (Stress Management, Self - Perception, Self-Expression, Interpersonal, and decision-making) as measured by EQ2.0-I (Bar-On, 1997)?

Hypothesis 3a (null): The fearful attachment style is not positively related to the stress management emotional intelligence subscales.

Hypothesis 3a (alternative): Fearful attachment style is positively related to the Stress management Emotional Intelligence subscale.

Hypothesis 3b (null): Fearful attachment style is not positively related to the decision-making emotional intelligence sub-scales.

Hypothesis 3b (alternative): Fearful attachment style positively affects the decision-making emotional Intelligence subscale.

Hypothesis 3c (null): Fearful attachment style is not positively related to the self-perception emotional intelligence sub-scales.

Hypothesis 3c (alternative): Fearful attachment style is positively related to the self-perception Emotional Intelligence subscale.

Hypothesis 3d(null): Fearful attachment style is not positively related to the interpersonal emotional intelligence sub-scales.

Hypothesis 3d (alternative): Fearful attachment style is positively related to the interpersonal Emotional Intelligence subscale.

Hypothesis 3e(null): Fearful attachment style is not positively related to the self-expression emotional intelligence sub-scales.

Hypothesis 3e (alternative): Fearful attachment style is positively related to the self-expression Emotional Intelligence subscale.

Research Question 4: Is there a significant relationship between preoccupied attachment style as measured by RSQ (Griffin & Batholomew, 1994) and emotional intelligence subscales (Stress Management, Self-Perception, Self-Expression, Interpersonal, and decision-making) as measured by EQ2.0-I (Bar-On, 1997)?

Hypothesis 4a (null): Preoccupied attachment style is not positively related to stress management emotional intelligence sub-scales.

Hypothesis 4a (alternative): Preoccupied attachment style is positively related to the Stress-management Emotional Intelligence subscale.

Hypothesis 4b (null): Preoccupied attachment style is not positively related to the Decision-Making emotional intelligence sub-scales.

Hypothesis 4b (alternative): Preoccupied attachment style is positively related to the Decision-Making Emotional Intelligence subscale.

Hypothesis 4c (null): Preoccupied attachment style is not positively related to the self-perception management emotional intelligence sub-scales.

Hypothesis 4c (alternative): Preoccupied attachment style is positively related to the self-perceptions Emotional Intelligence subscale.

Hypothesis 4d (null): Preoccupied attachment style is not positively related to the interpersonal emotional intelligence sub-scales.

Hypothesis 4d (alternative): Preoccupied attachment style positively relates to the interpersonal Emotional Intelligence subscale.

Hypothesis 4e (null): Preoccupied attachment style is not positively related to the self-expression emotional intelligence sub-scales.

Hypothesis 4d (alternative): Preoccupied attachment style positively relates to the self-expression Emotional Intelligence subscale.

Research Question 5: Will the total score of attachment style as measured by RSQ (Griffin & Batholomew, 1994) predicts emotional intelligence as measured by EQI-2.0 (Bar-On, 1997) based on moderating effects of age, gender, and race?

Hypothesis 5 (null): Attachment style as measured by RSQ (Griffin & Bartholomew, 1994) does not predict emotional intelligence as measured by EQI-2.0 (Bar-On, 1997) based on moderating effects of age, gender, or race.

Hypothesis 5 (alternative): Attachment style as measured by RSQ (Griffin & Bartholomew, 1994) predicts emotional intelligence as measured by EQI-2.0 (Bar-On, 1997) based on moderating effects of age, gender, or race.

Hypothesis 5A (null): Attachment style as measured by RSQ (Griffin & Batholomew, 1994) does not predict emotional intelligence as measured by EQI-2.0 (Bar-On, 1997) based on moderating effects of age.

Hypothesis 5A (alternative): Attachment style, as measured by RSQ (Griffin & Batholomew, 1994), predicts emotional intelligence, as measured by EQI-2.0 (Bar-On, 1997), based on the moderating effects of age.

Hypothesis 5B (null): Attachment style, as measured by RSQ (Griffin & Batholomew, 1994), does not predict emotional intelligence, as measured by EQI-2.0 (Bar-On, 1997), based on the moderating effects of gender.

Hypothesis 5B (alternative): Attachment style as measured by RSQ (Griffin & Batholomew, 1994) predicts emotional intelligence as measured by EQI-2.0 (Bar-On, 1997) based on moderating effects of gender.

Hypothesis 5C (null): Attachment style, as measured by RSQ (Griffin & Batholomew, 1994), does not predict emotional intelligence, as measured by EQI-2.0 (Bar-On, 1997), based on the moderating effects of race.

Hypothesis 5C (alternative): Attachment style, as measured by RSQ (Griffin & Batholomew, 1994), predicts emotional intelligence, as

measured by EQI-2.0 (Bar-On, 1997), based on
the moderating effects of race.
The present study's independent variable (IV) is
attachment style and the attachment style subscales:
secure, dismissive, preoccupied, and fearful. The present
study's dependent variable (DV) is the Emotional
Intelligence and Emotional Intelligence subscales: stress
management, self-perception, self-expression,
interpersonal, and decision-making.
Levels: Age, Sex, Race, and Sexual Orientation.

Research Design
      This research uses quantitative methodology and
a self-report survey method of data collection.
Participants are students ages 18 and up from U.S.
universities who receive survey links. The online version
has the informed consent form on the first page, where
participants learned that participation was voluntary
upon clicking the link. The students who participated
were then prompted to complete the Relationships
Scales Questionnaire (Griffin & Bartholomew, 1994),
which assessed individual differences in attachment
style. On the next page were the demographic questions,
and participants entered a four-digit PIN after the last
question. Participants were informed to use the same 4-
digit pin in the EQ-I-2.0 link in the "Name" section of
the EQi 2.0. The EQi 2.0 MHS portal was contacted to
purchase the scored datasets. The data was downloaded
in Excel format. The data was then paired with the RSQ
data and demographic with other survey data using the
4-digit identification number.

The EQ-2.0 and RSQ hinged on the five-point Likert scale, with one standing for "not at all" and five at the other end standing for "very likely." The surveys contained about 150 questions and took approximately 20 minutes to complete. After completing the study, the researcher thanked the participants.

Sampling Design

The population considered are students in universities and colleges in the U.S. Participants are enrolled in an undergraduate or graduate program and are at least 18 years of age. The survey was conducted in English only. The minimum required sample size was 115 participants, according to a G Power analysis. With a confidence interval of 95% and a $p = .05$, one can anticipate a medium effect size ($f=.15$). This sampling requirement was derived from an <u>F-test</u> using multiple regression analysis accounting for five predictor variables. The sample size was increased by 20% to account for refusals, missing data, or adjustments for confounding factors (Matinez-Mesa et al., 2014), resulting in an ideal minimum sample of 138 participants.

Recruitment

Recruitment consisted of various procedures—one method involved using the https://psych.hanover.edu/research/exponnet.html website to recruit participants. In addition, the participants were recruited through friends' emails, who could forward the survey links to people who have college student contacts via email and post them on their Instagram account, LinkedIn, and Facebook.

Procedures

The survey used EQ-I-2.0, RAQS, and demographic questions. The sample is from students who agreed to participate after receiving a brief introduction to the research with an online link. The survey was conducted for all university and college students eighteen or older. Additionally, the participants received an explanation of the nature of the research and its purpose. Participation in the study was voluntary and confidential without collecting personal identification, such as name and contact information. At the beginning of the survey, participants were e aware that they could stop anytime and that there was no time limit for completing the survey. The survey also provided a cautionary note to participants about possibly experiencing fatigue during the survey process.

An independent scoring agent collects and analyzes the data retrieved from the EQ-i2.0. This researcher purchased the processed data for EQi2.0 and conducted further analyses of the data. This researcher analyzes EQi2.0 and retrieves and analyzes the SurveyMonkey data. The researcher secured both survey data. They were kept in a locked file, after which data analysis with IBM SPSS (v.29) software for statistical analyses of the data was conducted.

Measures and Data Collection: The survey consisted of a 30-item Relationships Scales Questionnaire (RSQ) for the attachment style questionnaire, which was used to calculate four attachment styles: secure, preoccupied, dismissing, and fearful—the EQi-2.0 measures emotional intelligence with 116 self-report questions. The survey also included ten demographic questions.

The Relationships Scales Questionnaire (RSQ) (Griffin & Bartholomew, 1994)

The RSQ determines participants' attachment styles. The RSQ used a Likert-type scale that measured the study's four attachment styles. The RSQ contained 30 short statements; five addressed the dismissing and secure attachment patterns, and four pertained to the preoccupied and fearful attachment styles. The instrument comprised questions about the participants' close relationship and what best describes their relationship; for example, "I find it difficult to depend on other people," participants chose from a five-point Likert-type scale.

The RSQ instrument rates the extent to which a statement describes the characteristics of the participants' attachment styles. Five statements represented secure and dismissive attachments; four questions represented each of the other three attachment styles. The RSQ is a continuous measure of adult attachment. Secure attachment style included items 3,9,10, 15, and 28; the fearful/avoidance attachment style included items 1, 5, 12, and 24. The preoccupied attachment style included items 6, 8, 16, and 25, and the dismissing attachment style included items 2, 6, 19, 22, and 26. Reverse scoring was computed for items 9, 28, and 6 (Grifin & Bartholomew, 1994). The means of the score for each subscale represents the score of each subscale, where the highest score of the subscales represents the attachment style of the participants (Grifin & Bartholomew, 1994).

The Psychometric Properties of the Relationship Scale Questionnaire

The internal consistencies of the two dimensions of avoidance and anxiety were 0.85 to 0.90, which shows high reliability. The retest reliability of the RSQ ranged from 0.54 to 0.78, and the correlation coefficient of the RSQ ranged from 0.41 to 0.61 (Grifin & Bartholomew, 1994). The discriminant validity of the RSQ showed that there is a lack of discriminant validity with an HTMT (Heterotrait-monotrait) value higher than 0.85 and Cronbach's alpha of .85 and .81 for avoidance and anxiety, respectively (Zortea et al., 2019).

The Bar-On Emotional Quotient Inventory (EQi-2.0)

The EQ-i-2.0 measured the five subscales of emotional intelligence by Dr. Reuven BarOn, which contains fifteen competencies divided into five sections that include interpersonal, decision-making, stress management, self-perception, and self-expression, and also consisted of the interpretation by a certified administrator (The Emotional, 2023)—developing competencies based on the fifteen competencies: self-regard, self-actualization, emotional self-awareness, emotional expression, assertiveness, independence, interpersonal relationships, empathy, social responsibility, problem-solving, reality testing, impulse control, flexibility, stress tolerance, and optimism (Bar-On, 1997). The fifteen competencies are measured because each subscale measures different skills. For example, the ability to possess strong interpersonal skills is not the same as the ability to be aware of oneself. The Eq-I 2.0 also gives the inventory of a well-being indicator that shows the big picture of the participant's life (The Emotional, 2023).

The EQi-2.0 Psychometric Properties

An Analysis of variance (ANOVA) determines the effect of gender on EQ-I scores (Bar-On et al., 2000). EQ-I is an earlier version of EQ-2.0. Therefore, they share similar psychometric properties. The older group tends to score more than the younger group, with respondents in their early forties and early fifties having the highest mean score. There was no difference in the mean scores between males and females; for overall emotional and social competencies, males had more vital intrapersonal skills than females, and females had stronger interpersonal skills than males (Bar-On et al., 2000). The intercorrelation of the subscales was 0.19, which means that the subscales are not firmly socially biased and are independent, contributing uniquely to the measure, and the average correlation of the 15 subscales was 0.50, which shows the expected high intercorrelation between the factors (Bar-On et al., 2000).

The internal consistency of EQ-I showed an average Cronbach alpha coefficient for all subscales from 0.69 to 0.86 and average internal consistency of 0.76, which showed the instrument has excellent reliability (Bar-On et al., 2000). The test-retest reliability was 0.73 after a group of young adults were retested after four months (Bar-On, 1997b). The theoretical basis of the EQ-I is to determine the extent to which the EQ-I measures are theoretically justified. The exploratory factor analysis based on two individual EQ-I subscales (empathy and social responsibility) had a high correlation factor of 0.80. Validation of the EQ-I examines how adequately the instrument measures what to measure. EQ-I construct validity compared with the Attribution style questionnaire (Seligman et al., 1979), Beck depression inventory (Beck & Steer, 1987), coping inventory for stressful situations (Endler &Parker, 1990), and many others (Bar-On et al., 2000).

The EQ-I emotional and social intelligence construct validity, which is awareness, understanding, control, and express emotions r=0.36, emotional stoop test (Parker, 1999) r=0.72, TAS-20 total score (Parker et al., forthcoming) r= -0.44. SIFA total score (Dawda & Hart, 2000) r=0.58, and TMMS total score (Henner, 1998) = +0.46, the core components of emotions and social intelligence (Bar-On et al., 2000). The subscales construct validity for EQ-I self-regard subscale and PAI borderline features scale (Bar-On, 1997b) has a high negative correlation of
-.74. The Emotional self-awareness subscale for EQ-I had a positive correlation of +.33 with the ES subscale and emotional Stroop task (Parker, 1999) which shows that this subscale measures emotional awareness (Bar-On et al., 2000).

Assertiveness subscales of EQ-I had a high correlation of +.60 with the 16PF Factor E (Bar-On, 1997b), revealing that the assertiveness subscale measures the ability to be assertive and express oneself (Bar-On et al., 2000). The empathy subscale of EQ-I had r=+0.42 with the TMMS Clarity of Feelings Scale (Henner, 1998). The interpersonal Relationship of the EQ-I subscale positively correlated +.44 with the Emotional Stroop Task (Bar-On et al., 2000). The stress tolerance subscale of EQ-I had a positive correlation of +0.62 with the TMMS clarity of feelings scale (Henner,1998), impulse control measured by Eq-I IC subscale had r=0.50 with TMMS Clarity of feelings scale (Henner,1998), Reality testing measured by EQ-I RT subscale measures what it supposed to measure with a r=+0.58 with 16PF Factor C (Bar-On, 1997b) (Bar-On et al., 2000).

Flexibility measured by EQ-I Fl subscale had a moderate correlation with POI EX (+.35) and Sy (+.35) scales (Bar-On, 1997b), problem-solving measured by EQ-I PS Subscale correlated r=+0.41 with the TMMS Clarity of Feelings Scale (Henner, 1998) (Bar-On et al., 2000). Optimism measured by the EQ-I OP subscale had r=+0.55 with TMMS Mood Repair Scale (Henner, 1998), and Self-Actualization measured by the EQ-I SA subscale had r=+.44 with factor C on NEO (Dawda & Hart, 2000; Bar-On et al., 2000). Happiness measured by the EQ-I HA subscale had r=+0.61 with 16PF Factor E and r=+0.50 with 16PF Factor F (Bar-On, 1997b), Independence measured by EQ-I IN subscale r=+0.46 16PF Factor C, social responsibility measured by EQ-I RE subscale had r=+0.48 with TMMs clarity of feelings scale (Henner, 1998). Divergent validity, the effort of something not being what it is supposed to be, was obtained with a correlation of 0.12 between EQ scores and IQ scores, which shows that EQ did not measure IQ (Bar-On et al., 2000).

Table 4

Variables and Statistical Analyses by Research Question

Hypothesis	IV	DV	Moderating Variable	Statistical Test
H1a:	Secure attachment style	Self-perception	N/A	Linear Regression
H1b:	Secure attachment style	Self-expression	N/A	Linear Regression
H1c:	Secure attachment style	Interpersonal	N/A	Linear Regression
H1d:	Secure attachment style	Decision-Making	N/A	Linear Regression
H1e:	Secure attachment style	Stress management	N/A	Linear Regression
H2a	Dismissive attachment style	Self-perception	N/A	Linear Regression
H2b	Dismissive attachment style	Self-expression	N/A	Linear Regression

H2c	Dismissive attachment style	Interpersonal	N/A	Linear Regression
H2d	Dismissive attachment style	Decision-Making	N/A	Linear Regression
H2e	Dismissive attachment style	Stress management	N/A	Linear Regression
H3a	Fearful attachment style	Self-perception	N/A	Linear Regression
H3b	Fearful attachment style	Self-expression	N/A	Linear Regression
H3c	Fearful attachment style	Interpersonal	N/A	Linear Regression
H3d	Fearful attachment style	Decision-Making	N/A	Linear Regression
H3e	Fearful attachment style	Stress management	N/A	Linear Regression
H4a	Preoccupied attachment style	Self-perception	N/A	Linear Regression
H4b	Preoccupied attachment style	Self-expression	N/A	Linear Regression

H4c	Preoccupied attachment style	Interperso nal	N/A	Linear Regression
H4d	Preoccupied attachment style	Decision- Making	N/A	Linear Regression
H4e	Preoccupied attachment style	Stress manageme nt	N/A	Linear Regression
H5a	Attachment Style	Emotional Intelligenc e	Age	Moderated Multiple Regression
H5b	Attachment Style	Emotional Intelligenc e	Gender	Moderated Multiple Regression
H5c	Attachment Style	Emotional Intelligenc e	Race	Moderated Multiple Regression

Ethical Considerations

The researcher obtained permission from the Internal Review Board (IRB) of Keiser University before conducting the research for the safety of participants. Also, there were no expected financial benefits from the result of this study, and the researcher was not a participant in the study. Also, the interaction between participants and researchers is limited due to anonymous and online research. Participation was voluntary, and participants could withdraw from the study at any time. The researcher stored the collected data in a locked file to protect participants.

CHAPTER 4

Data Analysis and Results

This chapter will describe the sample, the sampling process, all pertinent demographic information, and the results of the five research questions and sub-questions. Because this was a quantitative study, all statistical methods used and reasoning for their use in the analysis will be discussed. The purpose of these results will be to further understand the relationship(s) between attachment styles and emotional intelligence.

Interpretation of Measures

The Relationship Scales Questionnaire (RSQ): The RSQ calculates attachment-style subscales by adding the items from the Secure attachment style, including items 3,9,10, 15, and 28; the fearful/avoidance attachment style included items 1, 5, 12, and 24. The preoccupied attachment style included items 6, 8, 16, and 25, and the dismissing attachment style included items 2, 6, 19, 22 and 26. Reverse scoring was computed for items 9, 28, and 6 before computing the scores for each subscale (Grifin & Bartholomew, 1994). The means of the score for each subscale represents the score of each subscale, and the highest score of the subscale represents the attachment style of the participants (Grifin & Bartholomew, 1994).

The RSQ attachment style subscale ranged from 8.10 (M=11.77, SD=2.27), meaning the participants had a medium attachment style. The RSQ is divided into four attachment styles, which include secure, dismissive, preoccupied, and fearful. The RSQ also included other variables of the subscales, which include relationship worry items 11, 12, 21, 23, closeness items 3, 4, 30, independence items 1, 2, 19, 26, fear of separation Items 8,9, 14, 25, 28, avoidance Items are 6,13,20, 24, 29, and anxiety items are 9, 11, 16, 21, 23, 25, 28

The Bar-On Emotional Quotient Inventory (EQi-2.0): The EQi-2.0 presents the results as standard scores and was adjusted by comparing them to the results of other participants. The scores are calculated with an average score of 100 and a standard deviation of 15, which allows one to know where the participant score is compared to the standard group. The diagram below shows the descriptive statistics of emotional intelligence. The total EI score is created by adding 118 of the 133 items, which shows whether the individual can perceive, express, develop, and maintain social relationships. The EQi-2.0 range was 217 (M=424.02, SD=45.74), meaning the participants showed moderate emotional intelligence. The EQi-2.0 has five emotional intelligence subscales: interpersonal, self-perception, self-expression, decision-making, and stress management. The EQi-2.0 subscales also included Interpersonal EI, interpersonal relationships, empathy, and social responsibility. Self-perception EI includes self-regard, self-actualization, and emotional self-awareness; self-expression EI includes emotional expression, assertiveness, and independence. The stress management of EI subscale includes flexibility, stress tolerance, and optimism, and the Decision-making subscale includes problem-solving, reality testing, and impulse control.

Table 5

Descriptive statistics and Cronbach's alpha for the RSQ and EQi-2.0

Instrument	Range	M	SD	a	Kurtosis
RSQ	8.10	11.77	2.27	0.72	-1.29
EQi-2.0	217.00	424.02	45.74	0.81	1.14

M=mean score of the sample, SD=standard deviation of the scores, a=internal consistency.

Descriptive Statistics

There were 386 participants in the RSQ and demographic surveys, and 186 completed the EQi-2.0 survey. 140 EQi-2.0 included PINS for identification, 122 participants were included in the study because duplicated PINs and incomplete surveys were removed. The 122 participants include males (n = 71, 58.2%) and females (n = 51, 41.8%). The age group was 18 to 48, with a mean of 28.21 and a standard deviation of 5.55. The participants include whites (n = 65, 53.3%), blacks (n =48, 39.3%), Hispanic (n = 4, 3.3%), Asian (n = 1, 0.8%), native American (n = 2, 1.6%), native Hawaiians (n = 1, 0.8%), and other races (n = 1, 0.8%).

Other demographics collected in this study include participants' current education levels: associate degrees (n = 18, 28.1%), bachelor's degrees (n =37,

57.8%), master's degrees (n = 6, 9.4%), and other (n = 3, 4.7%). The participant's employment status was part-time (n = 33, 51.6%), employed full-time (n = 24, 37.5%), unemployed (n = 6, 9.4%), and preferred not to answer (n = 1, 1.6%). The family composition of the participants was nuclear families (n = 45, 70.3%), single families (n = 8, 12.5%), stepparents (n = 5, 7.8%), grandparent (n = 4, 6.3%), and other (n = 1, 1.6%).

Summary of the Results

Table 6

Descriptive Statistics of Age of Participants

Variable	Mean	Std. Deviation	Range
Age	28.21	5.55	30

Table 7

Descriptive Statistics of the Frequences of Covariances

Variables	**Percent**
Gender	
Male	58.2%
Female	41.8%
Enrolled	
Part-time	39.3%
Full time	41.0%
Not at all	19.7%
Prefer not to say	

Race
  White   53.3%
  Black   39.3%
  Hispanic   3.3%
  Asian   0.8%
  Native American   1.6%
  Native Hawaiian   1.6%
Education
  Associate   22.1%
  Bachelors   55.7%
  Masters   18.7%
  Other   1.6%
Ethnicity
  Hispanic   6.6%
  Not Hispanic   90.2%
  Prefer not to say   2.5%
  Others   0.8%
Family type
  Nuclear   79.5%
  Single   8.2%
  Stepparent   6.6%
  Extended   4.9%
  Grandparent   0.8%
  Other

Employed
  Part-time   51.6%
  Full time   40.2%
  Not at all   8.2%
  Prefer not to answer

Missing Data and Outliers

After collecting the data, the missing data is investigated using frequency counts. The total number of participants from both RSQ and demographics was 386, and the EQi-2.0 had 186 participants. 140 participants included PINS to merge the two surveys. However, 18 participants had data missing in their demographic sections, completed less than 50% of the RSQ questionnaire, and were eliminated. The RSQ had missing data, two missing data from the 122 participants included in the study, and a mean score was calculated and input as the response suggested by Scheffer, 2002. The data analysis in this study was conducted without missing data. Outliers were identified using boxplots for RSQ and EQi-2.0. The z-scores for all the variables were calculated to verify the extreme values. The RSQ total score box plot had three outliers, and the EQi-2.0 box plot had eight outliers; the z scores for the outliers were under 3, so they were not removed.

Figure 4

Boxplot of RSQ Total Sore for All Participants

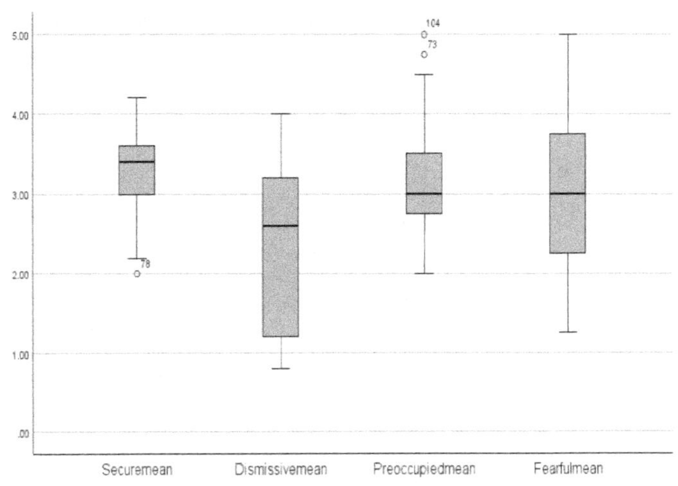

Figure 5

Boxplot of EQi-2.0 Total Score for All Participants

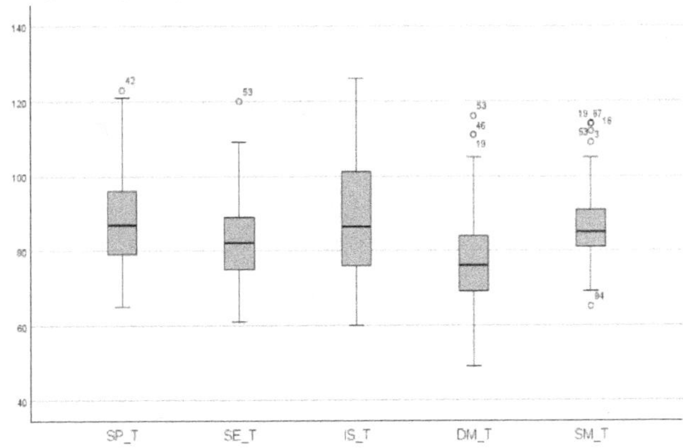

The Normality Test

The normality test was the assumption used to evaluate the dataset and ensure it complies with the assumption of normal distribution. The Shapiro -Wilk test evaluates the null hypothesis that a data sample is from a normal distribution.

Table 8

Normality test using Shapiro-Wilk

Variables	Shapiro-Wilk		
	Statistic	df	Sig.
Self-Perception	.968	122	.005
Self-Expression	.972	122	.013
Interpersonal	.980	122	.073
Decision Making	.972	122	.011
Stress Management	.942	122	<.001
Secure	.966	122	.004
Dismissive	.885	122	<.001
Preoccupied	.965	122	.003
Fearful	.957	122	<.001
Relationship Worries	.980	122	.063
closeness	.919	122	<.001
Independence	.897	122	<.001
Fear of Separation	.963	122	.002
Avoidance	.939	122	<.001
Anxiety	.939	122	<.001

The above table shows that interpersonal and relationship worries were normally distributed. However, because the Sig. value of the Shapiro-Wilk

Test is greater than 0.05, and sig. below 0.05, the data significantly deviates from a normal distribution.

Procedure

Correlation analysis was used to measure the correlation between attachment styles and emotional intelligence abilities. Regression analysis was used to measure the predictive level of attachment styles on emotional intelligence abilities. SPSS version 29 was used for data analysis.

Results

The EQi-2.0 and RSQ subscales were analyzed by obtaining their descriptive statistics, correlation analyses, and regression analyses. The regression analysis examined the predictive level of attachment styles on emotional intelligence abilities, as shown below.

Table 9

Mean, Standard Deviation, Confidence Intervals of EQi-2.0, and the RSQ Sub-scales.

		N	Mean	Std. Deviation	Confidence Intervals	
					Lower	Upper
Attach ment Styles	Secure	122	3.34	0.44	3.26	3.42
	Preoccupie d	122	3.15	0.63	3.04	3.26

		122	2.32	0.98	2.15	2.50
	Dismissing	122	2.32	0.98	2.15	2.50
	Fearful	122	2.95	0.91	2.79	3.12
Emotional Intelligence	Self-Perception	122	88.73	13.18	86.37	91.09
	Self-Expression	122	82.88	10.33	81.03	84.73
	Interpersonal	122	88.89	15.27	86.16	91.63
	Decision Making	122	77.02	12.13	74.85	79.20
	Stress Management	122	86.49	9.18	84.85	88.14
Other Attachment Styles variables	Relationship worries	122	3.44	0.60	3.33	3.55
	Closeness	122	3.81	0.88	3.65	3.97
	Independence	122	2.85	1.18	2.65	3.07
	Fear of Separation	122	3.35	0.64	3.23	3.46
	Avoidance	122	2.85	0.79	2.71	2.99
	Anxiety	122	3.53	0.63	3.41	3.64

The scores from RSQ and EQi-2.0 showed a positive relationship, while the higher RSQ scores showed a higher level of the attachment style subscale. The confidence intervals showed lower and upper confidence intervals.

Results of Relationship between Attachment Style Subscales and Emotional Intelligence Subscales

Table 10

Correlation Between Attachment Styles and Emotional Intelligence

Variables	Self - Perception	Self - Expression	Inter- personal	Decision Making	Stress Management
Secure	.044	-.051	.069	.078	.025
Preoccupied	.396**	-.032	.418**	-.111	.127
Dismissive	.587**	.189*	.581**	.222*	.204*
Fearful	.561**	.073	.542**	.185*	.160
Relationship worries	.011	-.208*	.083	-.162	-.033
Closeness	-.314**	-.194*	-.212*	-.240**	-.001
Independence	.570**	.059	.561**	.178	.133
Fear of Separation	-.046	-.281**	.055	-.387**	-.068
Avoidance	.500**	.043	.513**	.102	.186*
Anxiety	-.242**	-.319**	-.154	-.323	-.121

**Correlation is significant at the 0.01 level (2-tailed)
*Correlation is significant at the 0.05 level (2-tailed)
The correlation between total emotional intelligence subscale and total attachment subscales was .486**

The table above shows that secure attachment styles are significantly related to self-perception intelligence, interpersonal intelligence, decision-making, and stress management intelligence. Preoccupied intelligence also showed a positive relationship to self-perception intelligence, interpersonal and stress management, and a negative relationship to self-expression and decision-making. Dismissive and fearful attachment styles positively correlate to the five emotional intelligence subscales. Independence and avoidance were also positively related to the EQi-2.0 subscales, and closeness and anxiety were negatively related to the emotional intelligence subscales. Fear of separation was negatively related to the emotional intelligence subscale except interpersonal, which has a positive correlation. Also, relationship worries were positively correlated with two out of the five emotional intelligence subscales.

Table 11

Results of Regression Analyses Predicting Scores of Attachment Styles on Interpersonal Emotional Intelligence

Attachment Styles	R	R2	F	Beta	t
Secure	.62	.39	18.61	.16	2.111
Dismissive				.487	3.437
Preoccupied				-.007	-.066
Fearful				.16	1.145

Multiple regression was run to predict interpersonal emotional intelligence based on secure, fearful, dismissive, and preoccupied attachment styles. Results given in the Table above show that fearful, dismissing, secure, and preoccupied attachment styles combined have a significant effect on interpersonal emotional intelligence and account for 39% of the interpersonal emotional intelligence variance ($R = 0.62$, $R2 = 0.39$, $F (4-117) = 18.61$, $p < .01$). This model significantly predicts interpersonal emotional intelligence. Among the specific RSQ scales, dismissive attachment style ($\beta = .487$, secure ($\beta = .16$), and fearful ($\beta = .16$) were the predictors of interpersonal emotional intelligence ($p < .05$).

Table 12

Results of Regression Analyses Predicting Scores of Attachment Styles on Self-Perception Emotional Intelligence

Attachment Styles	R	R2	F	Beta	t
Secure	.62	.38	18.07	.10	1.29
Dismissive				.54	3.77
Preoccupied				-.05	-.48
Fearful				.13	.97

Results given in Table 12 show that attachment styles have a significant effect on self-perception emotional intelligence and account for 38% of the self-perception emotional intelligence variance ($R = 0.62$, $R2 = 0.38$, $F (4-117) = 18.07$, $p < .01$). This model significantly predicts self-perception emotional intelligence. Among the specific RSQ scales, the secure ($\beta = .10$) and dismissing attachment styles ($\beta = .38$) are the predictors of self-perception emotional intelligence ($p < .05$).

Table 13

Results of Regression Analyses Predicting Scores of Attachment Styles on Self-expression Emotional Intelligence

Attachment Styles	R	R2	F	Beta	t
Secure	.36	.13	4.24	-.14	-1.57
Dismissive				.59	3.47
Preoccupied				-.34	-2.76
Fearful				-.19	-1.18

Results given in the Table above show that attachment styles have a significant effect on self-expression emotional intelligence and account for 13% of the self-expression emotional intelligence variance (R = 0.36, R2 = 0.13, F (4-117) = 4.24, p < .01). This model significantly predicts self-expression emotional intelligence. Among the specific RSQ scales, the secure (β =- .14) and dismissive attachment styles (β = .59) are the predictors of self-expression emotional intelligence (p < .05).

Table 14

Results of Regression Analyses Predicting Scores of Attachment Styles on Stress-Management Emotional Intelligence

Attachment Styles	R	R2	F	Beta	t
Secure	.26	.07	2.19	-.03	-.27
Dismissive				.35	2.03
Preoccupied				-.10	-.81
Fearful				-.04	-.24

Results given in Table 5 show that the fearful, dismissing, secure, and preoccupied attachment styles combined have a significant effect on stress-management emotional intelligence (R = 0.26, R2 = 0.07, F (4-117) =2.19, p < .01). The attachment styles account for 7% of the stress management emotional intelligence variance. This model significantly predicts stress-management emotional intelligence. Among the specific RSQ scales, the dismissive (β = .35) and preoccupied attachment styles (β = -.10) are the predictors of stress-management emotional intelligence (p < .05).

Table 15

Results of Regression Analyses Predicting Scores of Attachment Styles on Decision Making Emotional Intelligence

Attachment Styles	R	R2	F	Beta	t
Secure	.45	.21	7.56	.01	.11
dismissive				.55	3.4
Preoccupied				-.51	-4.26
Fearful				.08	.48

p<.05.

Results given in the Table above indicate that the attachment styles have a significant effect on decision-making emotional intelligence (R = 0.45, R2 = 0.21, F (4-117) = 7.56, p < .01) and account for 21% of the decision-making emotional intelligence variance. This model significantly predicts decision-making emotional intelligence. Among the specific RSQ scales, the dismissive attachment style (β = .55) and preoccupied attachment style ($\beta = -.51$) are the main predictors of decision-making emotional intelligence ($p < .05$).

The regression analysis indicates that the total attachment styles have a significant effect on total emotional intelligence ($R = 0.49$, $R2 = 0.24$, $F (4-117) = 37.05$, $p < .01$) and account for 24% of the emotional intelligence variance. This model significantly predicts emotional intelligence. The RSQ scales of the attachment style ($\beta = .49$) are the main predictors of emotional intelligence ($p < .05$).

Table 16

Results of Regression Analyses Predicting Scores of Attachment Styles on Emotional Intelligence and Age as the moderator

Attachment Styles	R	R2	F	Beta	t
Attachment Style	.5	.25	19.61	.46	5.57
Age				-.11	-1.38
p<.05.					

Results given in Table 6 indicate that the attachment styles have a significant effect on emotional intelligence with the moderating effects of age ($R = .50$, $R2 = .25$, $F (2-119) = 19.61$, $p < .01$) and attachment style and age account for 25% of the emotional intelligence variance. This model significantly predicts emotional intelligence. The RSQ scales ($\beta = .46$) and the effect of age ($\beta = -.11$) are the predictors of emotional intelligence ($p < .05$).

Table 17

Results of Regression Analyses Predicting Scores of Attachment Styles on Emotional Intelligence and gender as the moderator

Attachment Styles	R	R2	F	Beta	t
Attachment Style	.50	.24	18.90	.47	5.6
gender				-.04	-.44

Results given in Table 16 indicate that the attachment styles have a significant effect on emotional intelligence with the moderating effects of gender (R = .5, R2 = .24, F (2-120) = 18.5, p < .01) and attachment style and gender account for 24% of the emotional intelligence variance. As a whole, this model significantly predicts emotional intelligence. The RSQ scales (β = .47) and the effect of gender (β = -.04) are the predictors of emotional intelligence (p < .05).

Table 18

Results of Regression Analyses Predicting Scores of Attachment Styles on Emotional Intelligence and race as the moderator

Attachment Styles	R	R2	F	Beta	t
Attachment Style	.49	.24	18.99	.48	6.05
Race				.09	1.10

p<.05.

Results given in Table 6 indicate that the attachment styles have a significant effect on emotional intelligence with the moderating effects of race (R = .49, R2 = .24, F

(2-118) = 18.99, p < .01) and account for 14.5% of the emotional intelligence variance. As a whole, this significantly predicts emotional intelligence. The RSQ scales (β = .48) and the effect of race (β =.09 are the predictors of emotional intelligence (p < .05).

Discussion of the Findings Based on Research Questions

According to the research findings, the total attachment style scores significantly predict emotional intelligence scores, which is consistent with Hamarta et al, 2009 and other findings.

According to the research findings, a positive correlation exists between secure attachment style and emotional intelligence: Stress Management, Self-perception, Interpersonal, and decision-making. The research showed a positive relationship between dismissive attachment and all the emotional intelligence subscales; dismissive attachment style had a positive relationship with interpersonal, self-expression, self-perception, decision-making, and stress management.

Preoccupied attachment style showed a positive relationship with self-perception, interpersonal and stress management, and negative relationships with self-expression and decision-making emotional intelligence subscales. The fearful attachment style showed a positive relationship with the emotional intelligence subscale. The research showed that a secure attachment style predicts stress management, self-perception, decision making, and interpersonal emotional intelligence. Based on this result, one can say that people with secure attachments have high interpersonal relationships, empathy, self-regard, self-esteem, and self-actualization compared to those with fearful, dismissing, and preoccupied attachment styles. This study shows that individuals with secure attachment styles have more self-confidence, self-determination, and problem-solving abilities that should be developed from childhood (Hamarta et al., 2009).

Scale Reliability

Cronbach's alpha measures data reliability or internal consistency, especially for Likert scale questionnaires like RSQ and EQi-2.0. The Cronbach alpha for the RSQ data was 0.72, indicating high internal consistency for the instrument compared to the RSQ, which ranged from 0.41 to 0.61 (Grifin & Bartholomew, 1994). The Cronbach alpha for the EQi-2.0 was 0.81, which also indicates high internal consistency compared to the EQi-2.0 Cronbach alpha of average Cronbach alpha coefficient for all subscales from 0.69 to 0.86 and average internal consistencies of 0.76 (Bar-On et al., 2000).

The Cronbach alpha coefficient of the RSQ is .72, though some of the subscales had negative coefficients. However, they had high split-half coefficients. The Cronbach alpha of dismissive attachment style was notably high at .876. The Cronbach alpha for the other attachment variables was high: closeness had a Cronbach alpha of .78, Independence had a Cronbach alpha of .92, fear of separation had a Cronbach alpha of .51, Avoidance .88, and anxiety Cronbach alpha of .67. The Cronbach alpha for the total EI was 0.81; for the individual scales, it was .76 for self-perception and .83 for interpersonal EI.

Exploratory Analysis

The histogram of the total EQi-2.0 graph represents the frequency of the participants' total scores. The histogram graph below reveals that most participants scored between 360 and 420, less than the mean score of 424.02, making the data distribution right skewed. Thus, 400 is the most frequently scored number, and the participants scored it 32 times.

Figure 6

Histogram of the Corresponding Total EQi-2.0 Sores

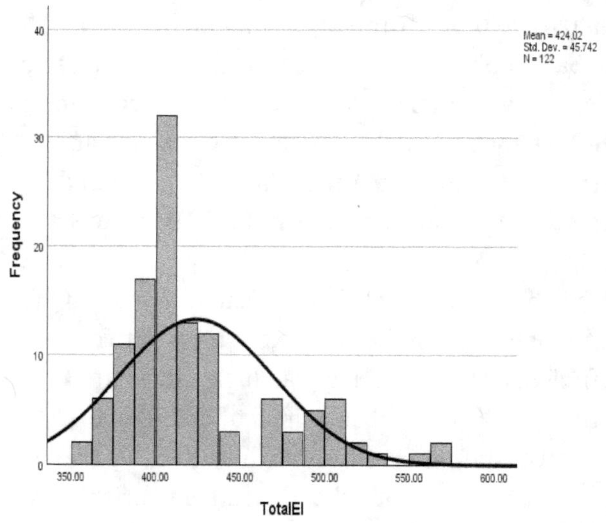

The histogram below shows the total RSQ scores of all participants. Although the histogram has almost all the scores in the center of the distribution, the frequency of the total score of 9 to 10 and 14 to 15 tends to occur more often than others, making the data bimodal.

Figure 7

Histogram of the Corresponding Total RSQ Scores

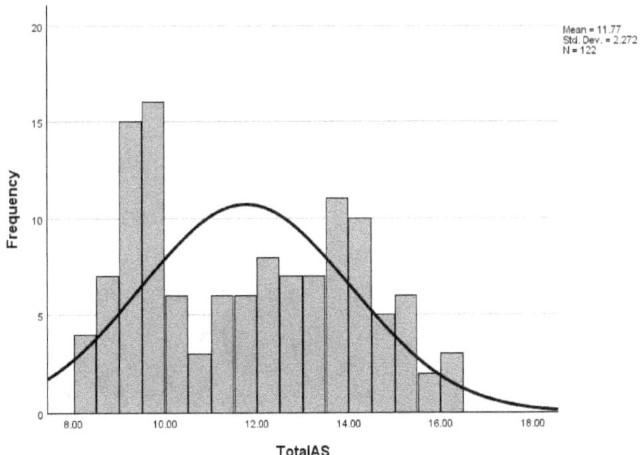

The scatterplot below shows the data from the total RSQ score and the total scores from the EQi-2.0. The data reveals the strength of the correlation between the total EQi-2.0 scores and the total RSQ scores. The scatterplot showed a significant scattering of points, with the points increasing in value from left to right. A line of best fit shows a linear relationship between EQi-2.0 and RSQ total scores.

Figure 8

99

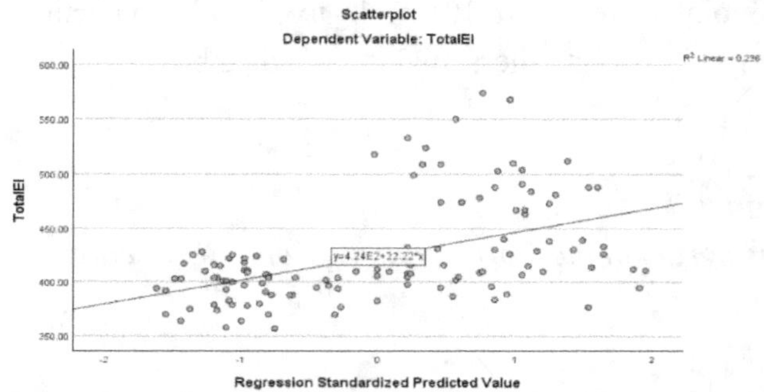

The line graph below helps to determine the relationship between male and female participants in the EQi-2.0 survey. The graph showed that the male participants scored higher than the female participants in most EQi-2.0 questions, though the scores appeared to be very close.

Figure 9

Line Graph Showing the Relationship Between Male and Female Participants in the EQi-2.0 Survey

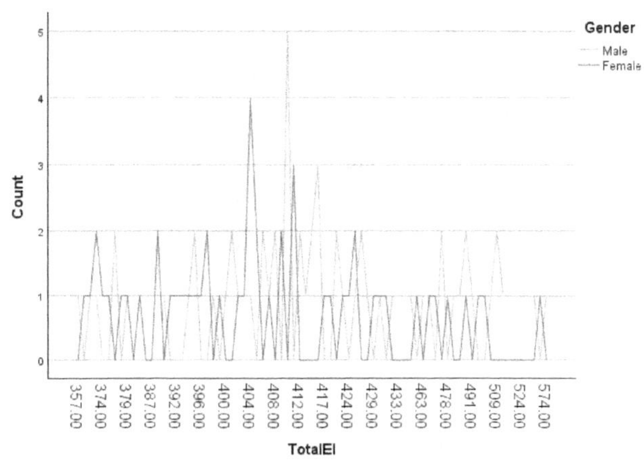

The line graph below helps to determine the relationship between male and female participants in the RSQ survey. The graph showed that the male participants scored higher than the female participants in most RSQ questions. This may be due to gender role upbringing that requires future in-depth exploration.

Figure 10

Line Graph Showing the Relationship Between Male and Female Participants in the RSQ Survey

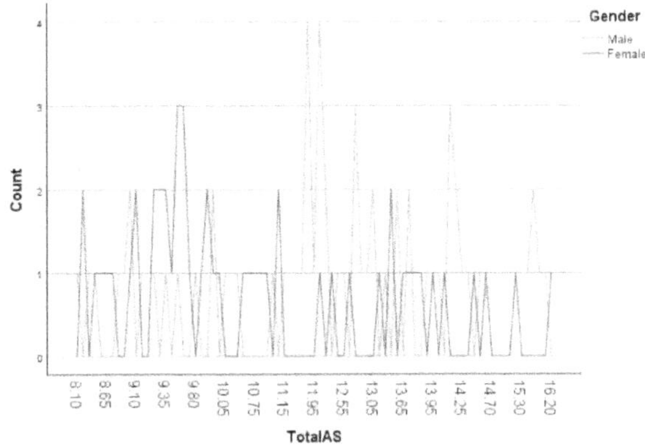

The line graph below helps to determine the relationship between the races of participants in the RSQ survey. The graph showed that the white participants scored higher than the other races in most RSQ questions, and the black participants had the second-highest score. This may be due to cultural differences, and further exploration is needed in future studies.

Figure 11

Line Graph Showing the Relationship Between Races of the Participants in the RSQ Survey

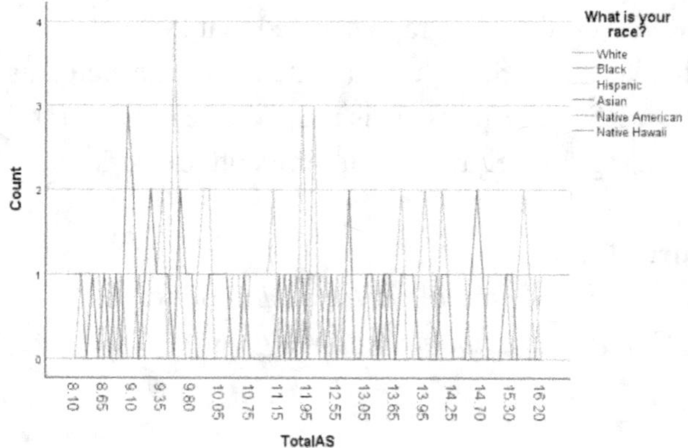

The line graph below helps to determine the relationship between the races of participants in the EQi-2.0 survey. The graph showed that the black participants scored higher than the other races in most EQi-2.0 questions, closely followed by the white participants. This may be due to cultural differences, and further exploration is needed in future studies.

Figure 12

*Line Graph Showing the Relationship Between Races of
the Participants in the EQi-2.0 Survey*

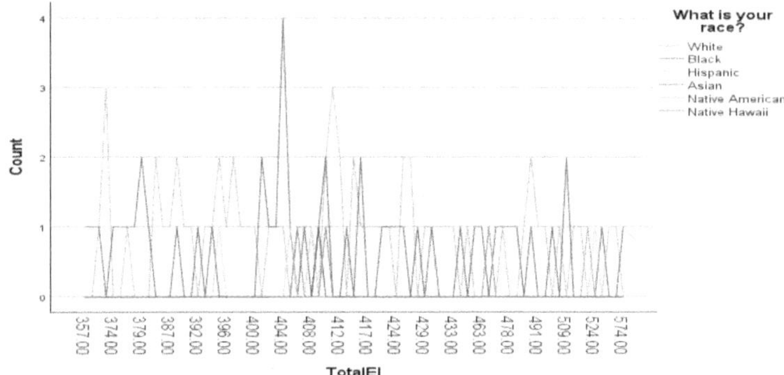

The line graph below helps to determine the
relationship between the age of participants in the EQi-
2.0 survey. The graph showed that most participants
between 27 and 31 years tended to have higher scores.
The frequency distribution of the age groups was
uneven across the line graph. This may be due to stages
of development, and further exploration is needed in
future studies.

Figure 13

*Line Graph Showing the Relationship Between Ages of
the Participants in the EQi-2.0 Survey*

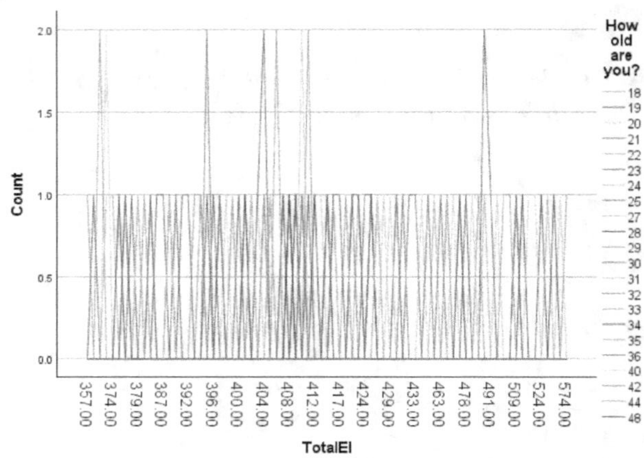

The line graph below helps to determine the relationship between the age groups of participants in the RSQ survey. The graph showed that participants ages 30, 28, and 24 tended to have higher scores; the frequency distribution of the ages was uneven across the line graph. This may be due to stages of development, and further exploration is needed in future studies.

Figure 14

Line Graph Showing the Relationship Between Ages of the Participants in the RSQ Survey

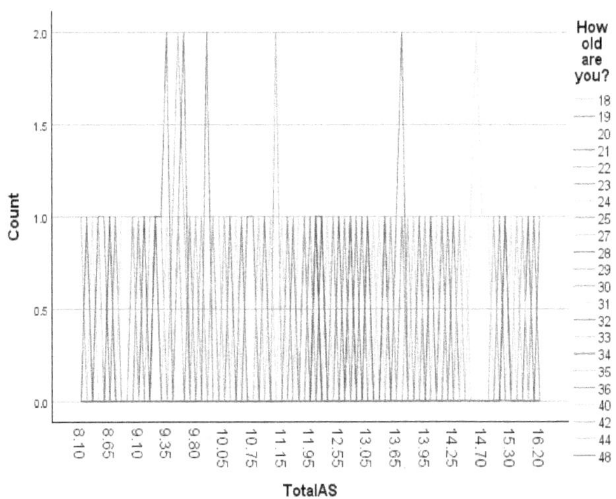

Correlation Analysis

The correlation analysis was conducted to determine the strength of the linear relationship between attachment styles and emotional intelligence associations. A positive correlation coefficient indicates that when there is an increase in the independent variable, there is a corresponding increase in the dependent variable. At the same time, a negative value shows an inverse relationship between the dependent and independent variables. The secure attachment style was related to most emotional intelligence factors, which positively correlate with stress management, self-expression, interpersonal skills, and decision-making. Dismissive attachment style had a positive relationship with the emotional intelligence subscales. Preoccupied attachment style showed a negative correlation with self-expression and decision-making and a positive relationship with self-perception, Interpersonal, and stress-management EI subscales.

Conclusion

This study examined the relationships between emotional intelligence and attachment style in college students. Although some null hypotheses were rejected, the participants reported moderate emotional intelligence and high attachment style scores. Furthermore, the EQi-2.0 histogram tends to be right-skewed, showing low emotional intelligence scores. The RSQ scores, on the other hand, were bimodal, showing that the participants had average RSQ scores. The scatter graph showed a linear relationship between the RSQ and EQi-2.0, which means that attachment style can predict emotional intelligence. The line graphs of the RSQ and EQi-2.0 with the covariances show a relationship between EQi-2.0 and RSQ due to the data intercepting each other at different points.

Chapter 5

Conclusions and Recommendations

This concluding chapter will touch on several topics. First, an overview of the study will be discussed. Then, the study's results will follow, exploring the results of the data analysis in the previous chapter. The study limitations will be examined and discussed, and where improvement could have been made, the last section will include recommendations for future research.

Overview of the Study

This study aims to better understand the relationship between emotional intelligence and attachment style. The ability of a person's attachment style to predict their emotional intelligence will go a long way toward helping people improve both their emotional intelligence and attachment style. EQi-2.0 was utilized to measure the participants' emotional intelligence and emotional intelligence subscales, and RSQ was used to measure the participants' attachment and attachment style subscales. The study by Scarlat, 2021 explained that attachment styles are significant predictors of emotional intelligence.

Discussion of the Results

Research Question 1: Is there a significant positive correlation between secure attachment style as measured by RSQ (Griffin & Batholomew, 1994) and emotional intelligence (Stress Management, Self - Perception, Self-Expression, Interpersonal, and decision-making) as measured by EQ2.0-I (Bar-On, 1997)?

A significantly positive predictor of emotional intelligence, associated with a higher level of emotional intelligence (Scarlat, 2021), and secure attachment predicted EI positively (Yahya et al., 2019).

Attachment styles are significant predictors of emotional intelligence. (Scarlat, 2021). Secure attachment positively predicted EI and a person with a secure attachment style have higher emotional intelligence (Yahya et al., 2019).

Hypothesis 1a (alternative): Secure attachment style is positively related to the self- perception subscales of emotional intelligence.

The result of the present study showed a positive relationship between secure attachment and self-perception; hence the alternative hypothesis is accepted that secure attachment style is positively related to self-perception and secure attachment style because securely attached individuals have self-regard, self-actualization, emotional self-awareness, which are the components of self-perception emotional intelligence (The Attachment Project, 2023). The regression analysis showed a significant positive relationship between secure attachment style and Stress Management, self-perception, Self-Expression, Interpersonal, and decision-making emotional intelligence. Therefore, the null hypothesis must be rejected.

Hypothesis 1b (alternative): Secure attachment style is positively related to the self-expression subscales of emotional intelligence.

The present study showed a nonsignificant negative relationship between self-expression and emotional intelligence. However, there should be a positive relationship between Self-expression and secure attachment style because securely attached individuals have emotional expression, assertiveness, and independence, which are the components of self-expression intelligence (The Attachment Project, 2023ject). Hamarta et al. 's 2009 study also revealed that secure attachment positively relates to self-expression subscales of emotional intelligence.

Hypothesis 1c (alternative): Secure attachment style is positively related to the interpersonal subscales of emotional intelligence.

The present study's results showed that a secure attachment style is positively related to interpersonal intelligence, confirmed in the studies of Yahya et al., 2019, and Hamarta et al., 2009, which found that secure attachment styles are positively related to the interpersonal emotional intelligence subscale. There is a positive relationship between interpersonal and secure attachment styles because securely attached individuals have interpersonal relationships, empathy, and social responsibility, which are the components of interpersonal intelligence (The Attachment Project, 2023)

Hypothesis 1d (alternative): Secure attachment style is positively related to the Decision-Making subscales of emotional intelligence.

The present study showed a positive relationship between decision-making emotional intelligence and secure attachment style. There is a positive relationship between decision-making and secure attachment style because securely attached individuals have problem-solving, reality testing, and impulse control, which are the components of decision-making emotional intelligence (The Attachment Project, 2023) Hypothesis 1e (alternative): Secure attachment style is positively related to emotional intelligence stress management subscales.

The present study revealed a positive relationship between stress management, emotional intelligence subscale, and attachment style. This confirmed the study of Yahya et al., 2019 and Hamarta et al., 2009 that a positive relation exists between stress management, emotional intelligence subscale and secure attachment style. There is a positive relationship between stress management and secure attachment style because securely attached individuals have flexibility, stress tolerance, and optimism, which are the components of stress management emotional intelligence (The Attachment Project, 2023).

This study's results are consistent with Hamarta et al.'s (2009) findings that there is a positive correlation between secure attachment and emotional intelligence. The correlational analysis showed that secure attachment is strongly related to stress management, self-perception, interpersonal, decision making and self-expression. This means that the person with a secure attachment will have self-regard, self-actualization, problem-solving skills, reality testing, emotional expression, interpersonal relationships, assertiveness, empathy, flexibility, independence, and impulse control (MHS). Therefore, there is a need to develop a secure attachment style from early childhood (Hamarta, 2009).

Research Question 2: Is there a significant correlation between Dismissive attachment style as measured by RSQ (Griffin & Batholomew, 1994) and emotional intelligence subscales (Stress Management, Self-Perception, Self-Expression, Interpersonal, and decision-making) as measured by EQ2.0-I (Bar-On, 1997)?

There are different findings on the relationships between dismissive or avoidant attachment style and emotional intelligence. A study revealed that dismissive attachment significantly predicts emotional intelligence (Scarlat, 2021). Others said dismissive attachment styles correlated negatively with emotional intelligence (Borawski et al., 2022). Dismissive attachment style and emotional awareness with a Pearson correlation value of -0.538 indicate strong negative correlations (Yahya et al., 2019), which stated a significant negative relationship between dismissive attachment and emotional awareness, which means that the strength of the relationship between avoidant attachment decreased with an increase in emotional intelligence (Yahya et al., 2019). When one has avoidant attachment, then he/she would have low emotional awareness, and the relationship found between the respondents' anxiety attachment scores and EI scores, although negative, was not statistically significant (p=0.19, r=0.332) (Fabella et al., 2023).

Hypothesis 2a (alternative): Dismissive attachment style is related to the Self- Expression Emotional Intelligence subscale.

The study showed a positive relationship between self-expression and emotional intelligence subscale. There is a positive relationship between Self-expression and dismissive attachment style because dismissive or avoidant attached individuals have emotional expression assertiveness and independence, which are the components of self-expression (The Attachment Project, 2023). This was also confirmed in the study of Hamarta et al., 2009.

Hypothesis 2b (alternative): Dismissive attachment style is related to the Decision-Making Emotional Intelligence subscale.

The study showed a positive relationship between dismissive attachment style and decision-making emotional intelligence subscale. There is a positive relationship between decision-making and dismissive attachment style because dismissive attached individuals have problem-solving, reality testing, and impulse control, which are the components of decision-making emotional intelligence (The Attachment Project, 2023)

Hypothesis 2c (alternative): Dismissive attachment style is related to the
Self-perception Emotional Intelligence subscale.

The result showed a significant positive relationship between dismissive attachment style and self-perception emotional intelligence. There is a positive relationship between self-perception and dismissive attachment style because dismissively attached individuals have self-regard, self-actualization, and emotional self-awareness, which are the components of self-perception emotional intelligence (The Attachment Project, 2023)

Hypothesis 2d (alternative): Dismissive attachment style is positively related to the Stress-management Emotional Intelligence subscale.

The result showed a significant positive relationship between dismissive attachment style and stress-management emotional intelligence subscale. There is a positive relationship between stress management and dismissive attachment style because dismissively attached individuals have flexibility, stress tolerance, and optimism, which are the components of stress management (The Attachment Project, 2023). The regression analysis showed a positive relationship between dismissive attachment and interpersonal, self-expression, and stress management and a negative relationship between dismissive attachment style and self-perception and decision-making emotional intelligence. Thus, the null hypothesis is rejected.

Hypothesis 2e (alternative): Dismissive attachment style positively relates to the interpersonal Emotional Intelligence subscale.

The result showed a positive relationship between dismissive attachment style and interpersonal emotional intelligence. However, the study of Hamarta et al., 2009 showed a negative relationship between dismissive attachment style and interpersonal emotional intelligence. There is a negative relationship between interpersonal and secure attachment styles because dismissively attached individuals do not have interpersonal relationships, empathy, and social responsibility, which are the components of interpersonal intelligence (The Attachment Project, 2023)

However, the dismissive attachment style positively correlates with interpersonal, self-expression, self-perception, decision-making, and stress management. This is not consistent with the findings of Hamarta et al. 2009, where dismissive attachment was positively correlated to three of the five emotional intelligence subscales. The dismissive attachment style is strongly correlated with interpersonal, stress management, and self-expression emotional intelligence.

Research Question 3: Is there a significant correlation between fearful attachment style as measured by RSQ (Griffin & Batholomew, 1994) and emotional intelligence subscales (Stress Management, Self - Perception, Self-Expression, Interpersonal, and decision-making) as measured by EQ2.0-I (Bar-On, 1997)?
Hypothesis 3a (alternative): Fearful attachment style positively relates to the Stress management Emotional Intelligence subscale.

The result of the fearful study showed an insignificant positive relationship between stress management and fearful attachment style. However, Hamarta et al., 2009 studies and other studies showed a negative relationship, the positiveness in this study may be due to the few participants. There should be a negative relationship between stress management and fearful attachment style because fearfully attached individuals do not have flexibility, stress tolerance, and optimism, which are the components of stress management (The Attachment Project, 2023) Hypothesis 3b (alternative): Fearful attachment style positively affects related to the decision-making emotional Intelligence subscale.

The result of the fearful attachment study showed an insignificant positive relationship between decision-making and fearful attachment style. However, Hamarta et al.'s 2009 studies and other studies showed a negative relationship, and the positivity in this study may be due to the small number of participants. There should be a negative relationship between decision-making and fearful attachment style because fearfully attached individuals do not have problem-solving, reality testing, and impulse control, which are the components of decision-making emotional intelligence (The Attachment Project, 2023). Hypothesis 3c (alternative): Fearful attachment style positively relates to the self-perception Emotional Intelligence subscale.

The result of the fearful study showed an insignificant positive relationship between self-perception and fearful attachment style. However, Hamarta et al.'s 2009 and other studies showed a negative relationship, and the positivity in this study may be due to the small number of participants. There should be a negative relationship between self-perception and fearful attachment style because fearfully attached individuals do not have self-regard, self-actualization, and emotional self-awareness, which are the components of self-perception (The Attachment Project, 2023)

Hypothesis 3d (alternative): Fearful attachment style positively relates to the interpersonal Emotional Intelligence subscale.

The fearful study showed an insignificant positive relationship between interpersonal and fearful attachment style. However, Hamarta et al., 2009 studies and other studies showed a negative relationship, the positivity in this study may be due to the few participants. There should be a negative relationship between the interpersonal emotional intelligence subscale and fearful attachment style because fearfully attached individuals do not have interpersonal relationships, empathy, and social responsibility which are the components of interpersonal intelligence (The Attachment Project, 2023).

Hypothesis 3e (alternative): Fearful attachment style positively relates to the self-expression Emotional Intelligence subscale.

The result of the fearful study showed an insignificant positive relationship between self-expression and fearful attachment style. However, Hamarta et al.'s 2009 and other studies showed a negative relationship, and the positivity in this study may be due to the small number of participants. There should be a negative relationship between self-expression and fearful attachment style because fearfully attached individuals do not have emotional expression, assertiveness and independence, which are the components of self-expression emotional intelligence (The Attachment Project, 2023)

The regression analysis showed a positive relationship between fearful attachment and interpersonal, self-expression, self-perception, decision-making, and stress management emotional intelligence. Therefore, the null hypothesis can be rejected. Hamarta et al. 2009, showed a negative correlation between fearful attachment style and all emotional intelligence subscales.

Research Question 4: Is there a significant correlation between preoccupied attachment style as measured by RSQ (Griffin & Batholomew, 1994) and emotional intelligence subscales (Stress Management, Self-Perception, Self-Expression, Interpersonal, and decision-making) as measured by EQ2.0-I (Bar-On, 1997)?

The preoccupied or anxious attachment style significantly negatively predicts emotional intelligence (Scarlat, 2021). Another research report that preoccupied attachment styles correlate negatively with EI (Borawski et al., 2022) is that the strength of the relationship between preoccupied attachments decreased with increased emotional intelligence. Emotional intelligence partially mediated the connection between anxious ambivalent attachment and predicted emotional intelligence negatively (Fabella et al., 2023). The result showed no significant relationship between anxious attachment and emotional management. Results of multiple regression analysis demonstrated that preoccupied attachment style in

teachers was the only predictor of the components of emotional intelligence (Kuhsar, 2018).
Hypothesis 4a (alternative): Preoccupied attachment style positively relates to the Stress-management Emotional Intelligence subscale.

The result of this study showed positive relationship between preoccupied attachment style and stress management. There is a negative relationship between stress management and preoccupied attachment style because preoccupied attached individuals do not have flexibility, stress tolerance, and optimism, which are the components of stress management (The Attachment Project, 2023)
Hypothesis 4b (alternative): Preoccupied attachment style is positively related to the
Decision-Making Emotional Intelligence subscale.

The study showed a negative relationship between preoccupied attachment style and decision-making emotional intelligence. However, the Hamarta et al., 2009 studies also showed a negative relationship. There should be a negative relationship between decision-making and preoccupied attachment style because preoccupied attached individuals do not have problem-solving, reality testing, and impulse control, which are the components of decision-making emotional intelligence (The Attachment Project, 2023)
Hypothesis 4c (alternative): Preoccupied attachment style is positively related to the self-perceptions Emotional Intelligence subscale.

The study showed a positive relationship between preoccupied attachment style and self-perception emotional intelligence. However, the

Hamarta et al., 2009 studies showed a negative relationship. There should be a negative relationship between self-perception and preoccupied attachment style because preoccupied attached individuals do not have self-regard, self-actualization, and emotional self-awareness, which are self-perception components (The Attachment Project, 2023). The preoccupied, attached individual has low interpersonal skills and a high sense of social isolation.

Hypothesis 4d (alternative): Preoccupied attachment style positively relates to the interpersonal Emotional Intelligence subscale.

The present showed a positive relationship between interpersonal emotional intelligence and preoccupied attachment style. There is a positive relationship between interpersonal and preoccupied attachment styles because preoccupied attached individuals have positive interpersonal relationships, empathy, and social responsibility, which are the components of interpersonal intelligence (The Attachment Project, 2023)

Hypothesis 4d (alternative): Preoccupied attachment style positively relates to the self-expression Emotional Intelligence subscale.

There is a negative relationship between Self-expression and preoccupied attachment style because preoccupied attached individuals do not have emotional expression, assertiveness, and independence, which are the components of self-expression emotional intelligence (The Attachment Project, 2023)

Hypothesis 4e (alternative): Preoccupied attachment style positively relates to stress-management Emotional Intelligence subscale.

The study showed a positive relationship between stress management and preoccupied attachment style; however, the Hamarta et al. 2009 study showed a negative relationship between stress management and preoccupied attachment style. There is a negative relationship between stress management and preoccupied attachment style because preoccupied attached individuals do not have flexibility, stress tolerance, and optimism, which are the components of stress management emotional intelligence (The Attachment Project, 2023).

The regression analysis showed a negative relationship between preoccupied attachment style and decision-making, as well as stress management and emotional intelligence. Therefore, the null hypothesis can be rejected. The preoccupied attachment style in Hamarta et al. study had a positive relationship with interpersonal emotional intelligence, and so did this study. However, this study showed a positive relationship between preoccupied attachment style, self-perception, and stress management.

Research Question 5: Will the total score of attachment style as measured by RSQ (Griffin & Batholomew, 1994) predicts emotional intelligence as measured by EQI-2.0 (Bar-On, 1997) based on moderating effects of age, gender, and race?

Hypothesis 5 (alternative): Attachment style, as measured by RSQ (Griffin & Batholomew, 1994), predicts emotional intelligence, as measured by EQI-2.0 (Bar-On, 1997), based on the moderating effects of age, gender, or race.

The covariances also affected the participants' emotional intelligence and attachment style. There was a distinguished difference between male and female participants' EQi-2.0 and RSQ scores. The graph showed that male emotional intelligence is sometimes higher than female emotional intelligence, possibly due to gender role nurturing from childhood, which needs further research. The RSQ showed almost equal attachment patterns between male and female participants.

Hypothesis 5A (alternative): Attachment style, as measured by RSQ (Griffin & Batholomew, 1994), predicts emotional intelligence, as measured by EQI-2.0 (Bar-On, 1997), based on moderating effects of age.

The result of the moderation analysis examined the influence of attachment style and emotional intelligence ($R = .49$, $R2 = .24$, $F (1-120) = 37.05$, $p < .01$) on age ($R = .50$, $R2 = .25$, $F (2-119) = 19.61$, $p < .01$) added an interaction of 1%, which shows that age has a moderating effect on attachment style and emotional intelligence. Age also played a part in emotional intelligence and attachment style, showing a marked difference between the age groups. The difference in attachment style and emotional intelligence due to age is based on experience from a close relationship (The Attachment Project, 2023)

Hypothesis 5B (alternative): Attachment style, as measured by RSQ (Griffin & Batholomew, 1994), predicts emotional intelligence, as measured by EQI-

2.0 (Bar-On, 1997), based on the moderating effects of gender.

The result of the moderation analysis examined the influence of attachment style and emotional intelligence ($R = .49$, $R2 = .24$, $F (1\text{-}120) = 37.05$, $p < .01$) on gender ($R = .48$, $R2 = .24$, $F (2\text{-}119) = 18.50$, $p < .01$) added an interaction of 0.1%, which shows that gender has a moderating effect on attachment style and emotional intelligence. Females possess higher EI scores than male (Fabella et al., 2023) explained that females have higher anxiety attachment scores than males.
Hypothesis 51C (alternative): Attachment style, as measured by RSQ (Griffin & Batholomew, 1994), predicts emotional intelligence, as measured by EQI-2.0 (Bar-On, 1997), based on the moderating effects of Race.

The result of the moderation analysis examined the influence of attachment style and emotional intelligence ($R = .49$, $R2 = .24$, $F (1\text{-}120) = 37.05$, $p < .01$) on Race ($R = .49$, $R2 = .24$, $F (2\text{-}119) = 18.89$, $p < .01$) added an interaction of 0.1%, which shows that race has a moderating effect on attachment style and emotional intelligence. Race also showed a marked difference in the participants.

Limitation

This study has significant limitations. The sample size is relatively small, so the results are not generalizable to all college students in the U.S. According to the research conducted by the National Institute of Mental Health (2017) showed that 6 million Americans live with mental illness. 213 million people

have low emotional intelligence, and unlabeled emotions
are misunderstood, leading to irrational choices and
counterproductive actions (Legacy Place). The
participants in this study are so limited that the reliability
and generalization of the study will be small.

Another limitation is the method of data
collection. Since the survey is a self-report survey,
participants were asked to answer the questions honestly.
However, there is no guarantee that there were no
external influences, like social desirability bias or
misunderstanding questions on the surveys. It is also
possible that students intentionally or unintentionally put
down wrong answers so they can be socially desirable to
other students. Also, because the survey was accessible
on social media, participants tend to be well-educated
and have higher socioeconomic status. The survey may
not be accessible to students from low socioeconomic
status.

Another limitation is that the instrument may not
measure what it should. However, the instruments in
this study were selected because they were used in the
2009 study by Hamarta et al. and show high reliability
and validity.

Recommendations For Future Research

Due to limited research on attachment style and
emotional intelligence, the recommendation is to explore
this topic with more participants to generalize it,
including people from diverse backgrounds, making the
sample size more viable. Sampling bias occurred
because some population members were systematically

removed and multiple survey format options were not offered (Chen, 2021). To prevent sampling bias, a multiple survey format must be created to enable students with limited access to laptops and the Internet to participate in the survey.

During the exploratory analysis, some intriguing interactions were found in the covariances. These interactions include gender, race, and age. Males and females showed variances in emotional intelligence and attachment styles. This may be due to higher resiliency and is suggested for future studies. There are marked differences in the race and age group of the participants; these are all exciting new topics to explore. Future researchers should explore the interaction in this study in more detail and add to this research.

Conclusion

Secure attachment is a significant positive predictor of emotional intelligence and is associated with higher emotional intelligence (Scarlat, 2021). This study's findings showed that people with a secure attachment style would have higher emotional intelligence, people with a dismissive attachment style would have medium emotional intelligence and people with a preoccupied and fearful attachment style would have low emotional intelligence. However, the study confirmed that attachment style predicts emotional intelligence.

A child who grows up with secure attachment will develop positive feelings about himself and others. The securely attached child feels safe, seen, known, comforted, reassured, soothed, valued, and

supported to explore, and the child can predict the caregiver's response. (attached project). Signs of secure attachment in an adult relationship will be being able to regulate emotions in the relationship, being goal-oriented, bonding quickly, trusting easily, knowing what he wants, knowing his purpose, communicating needs effectively, feeling that he matters,
being comfortable with closeness, seek emotional support from partner and give emotional support to partner, explore when alone and comfortable with alone time, and have the solid reflective capacity in a relationship.

They have more accessible social contacts, intimate relationships, and bonding. They are aware of their emotional needs and can express them; they feel good by themselves and in relationships. They have a favorable view of themselves and others, warm, loving, lovable, and a positive view of their childhood. Parents with secure attachment styles can regulate their emotions, give children a compassionate environment, and empathize with their children.
The main characteristics of secure attachment styles are making social contacts easily, bonding with people, feeling good about relationships, feeling confident and balanced, having a solid sense of self, feeling good about self, warm, open, straightforward, and easygoing. A secure, attached person will be open to criticism, have strong self-reflection skills, be a team player,
be comfortable in committed relationships, feel good alone, prefer sexual activities in serious relationships, be able to trust and rely on others, be aware of his

emotions and can maintain and express emotions openly (The Attachment Project, 2023).

Dismissive attachment is usually caused by caregivers who are strict and emotionally distant, with no tolerance for emotional feelings, and expect a child to be tough. Dismissive attachment in adults may appear to be self-sufficient due to a low tolerance for emotional or physical intimacy; they are high achievers and have difficulty building lasting relationships. Healing from avoidant attachment can be achieved through therapy and a healthier outlook to a more secure attachment style (The Attachment Project, 2023).

People with dismissive attachment styles are usually happy with themselves and their accomplishments, social, easy-going, and fun to be around, thereby having lots of friends or sexual partners. They have high self-esteem and do not require emotional support from others because they invest in their professional development and have confidence in their success (The Attachment Project, 2023). The dismissive attachment style only engages in surface-level relationships, avoids strong relationships and closeness, and ends relationships because of their fear of closeness. Individuals with dismissive attachment styles should admit to a lack of emotional intimacy and make efforts to change and develop closer relationships with people and let them in. In the dismissive attachment style, individuals must learn to trust others, open up more in relationships, and understand their emotions (The Attachment Project, 2023).

Fearful or disorganized attachment is the most challenging attachment style to manage, which develops from childhood fear when the only caregiver is a source of fear. They do not trust themselves and others and are highly inconsistent, which can lead to mental health issues like mood disorders. The fearful attachment style may be caused by a child having or witnessing trauma, inconsistency, and unpredictable caregiver. The child then distances themselves from the caregiver as a protection method. Adults with fearful attachment styles lack coherence; However, they actively seek to be close to other people, they learn from experience that those closest to them are not to be trusted, so they reject proximity and affection and repeat the same patterns in all their relationships (The Attachment Project, 2023).

Adults with fearful attachments may find it challenging to open up and be vulnerable in relationships because they have a negative view of themselves and others. The fearful attachment style individual tends to act in difficult and intolerable ways, pushing their partners away and confirming their fear of rejection. They may have mood swings and create conflicts in relationships because they have problems understandably expressing their needs and emotions. The fearful, attached individuals believe they cannot rely on others to accept and love them, so they act suspiciously and are jealous of their partners. They overanalyze their partner's actions for fear of rejection, so they shut their emotions down and may be unfeeling and cold to their partner. They behave like they hate their partner and do not want them to leave.

Communication with a fearful attachment style must be clear and open, consistent, patient, understanding, listening to their concerns, gradually developing trust, and considering therapy. A person with a fearful attachment style will be more likely to act out sexually so they can connect without intimacy. A fearful, attached person needs to understand their triggers, react to triggers, and respond healthily. They need to identify irrational thoughts about themselves and their relationships to change their fearful attachment style to a more secure one.

Preoccupied attachment style developed from childhood due to inconsistent parenting that is mistuned (The The Attachment Project, 2023, 2023), which is characterized by low self-esteem, fear of abandonment, fear of rejection, and clinginess. Parents who have a preoccupied attachment style are likely to raise children with a preoccupied attachment style by transferring their behavior to the children. Other causes of anxious attachment style include physical and psychological abuse and early separation from the caregiver. They are sensitive to their partner's needs but may consider themselves not being love-worthy if their loved one rejects them or does not respond to their needs, so they need constant reassurance that they are love-worthy. They are highly emotional and depend on others. This also causes anxiety, stress, low life satisfaction, and unhappiness. A reassuring partner counteracts the fear of being alone or being rejected. Attachment style can be changed with a relationship with a securely attached partner that facilitates a sense of calmness, stability, and emotional closeness. Even though one cannot change one's past, one can change one's present by observing how one interacts with loved ones to recognize behavioral patterns in relationships and be mindful of them, self-flections, and analyzing childhood experiences.

People with preoccupied attachment styles seek a more vital need for support and doubt the availability of support; they cry for support, are not calmed by their partner's support, have intense reactions to threats, feel distressed and more negatively thought of, and are unable to cope with stressful issues, cope with emotion-focused strategies like ruminating, blaming themselves, wishful thinking and focusing on distress. Things of preoccupied or anxious attachment in children are very responsive and very sensitive to others' needs at their own expense; they become distressed when their parents leave and are hard to comfort when the parent returns. The adult with a preoccupied or anxious attachment style may have an anxiety disorder, attention deficit disorder, self-critical, and seek others' validation. Parents with preoccupied attachment styles tend to be over-involved in their child's emotional needs and are unable to multitask around their child (The Attachment Project, 2023).

Exploratory analysis was conducted to see if there were any other significant relationships between variables. The exploration analysis revealed that most participants scored less than 90 points in the EQi-2.0, and a score of 100 and above is regarded as high emotional intelligence by MHS. The exploratory analysis also showed a linear positive relationship between emotional intelligence and attachment style,

which shows that when emotional intelligence increases, attachment style also increases and vice versa.
Therefore, an improvement in a person's emotional intelligence will cause an improvement in his attachment style.

References

Ainsworth, M. D. S., Blehar, M. C, Waters, E., & Wall, S. (1978). Patterns of attachment: *A psychological study of the strange situation.* Hillsdale, NJ: Erlbaum.

Ainsworth Salter, M. D., Blehar, M. C., Waters, E., & Wall, S. (2014). *Patterns of attachment a psychological study of the strange situation.* Psychology Press.

Aranda López, M., García Domingo, M., Fuentes Gutiérrez, V., & Linares Martínez, R. (2022). Emotional intelligence and adult attachment: Effects on problematic smartphone usage. *Anales de Psicología, 38*(1), 36–45. https://doi.org/10.6018/analesps.463101

Ballester, A. M. J., de la Barrera, U., Schoeps, K., & Montoya-Castilla, I. (2022). Emotional factors that mediate the relationship between emotional intelligence and psychological problems in emerging adults. *Psicología Conductual, 30*(1), 249-267 *Psicología Conductual, 30*(1), 249-267. https://doi.org/10.51668/bp.8322113n

Bar-On, R. (2006). The Bar-On model of emotional-social intelligence (ESI). *Pricothema,* 18 (Suppl.), 13-25. PMID: 17295953.

Bar-On R. (1996). *The Emotional Quotient Inventory (EQ-i): A Test of Emotional Intelligence.* Toronto, ON: Multi-Health Systems. https://www.scirp.org/reference/referencespapers?referenceid=768114

Bar-On R. (1997a). *Bar-On Emotional Quotient Inventory: User's Manual.* Toronto, ON: Multihealth Systems.

Bar-On R. (1997b). *The Emotional Quotient Inventory (EQ-i): Technical manual.* Toronto, ON: Multi-Health Systems, Inc.

Bar-On, R. (2006). The Bar-On model of emotional-social intelligence (ESI). Pricothema, 18 (Supl.), 13-25. PMID: 17295953.

Bar-On R., & Parker. J.D.A. (2000). The Bar-On EQ-I: YV: Technical manual. Toronto, Canada: Multi-Health Systems.

Bar-On, R. (2012). Emotional quotient-inventory. *PsycTESTS Dataset.* https://doi.org/10.1037/t04985-000

Beasley, K. (1987). The Emotional Quotient. Mensa, May 1987, p25.

Beck, A. T., & Steer, R.A. (1987). Manual Beck Depression Inventory. San Antonio, TX: Psychological Corporation.

Beldoch, M. (1964). sensitivity to the expression of emotional meaning in three modes of communication. In *The communication of emotional meaning* (pp. 31–42). essay, McGraw-Hill.

Belot, R., Bouteloup, M., Bonnet, M., Parmentier, A., Magnin, E., Mauny, F., & Vuillier, F. (2021). Evaluation of Attachment Style and Social Support in Patients with Severe Migraine. Applications in Doctor-Patient Relationships and Treatment Adherence.

doi: 10.3389/fneur.2021.706639

PMCID: PMC8313122 PMID: 34322089

Benoit, D. (2004a). Infant-parent attachment: Definition, types, antecedents, measurement, and outcome. *Paediatrics & Child Health*, *9*(8), 541–545. https://doi.org/10.1093/pch/9.8.541

Benoit, D. (2004b). Infant-parent attachment: Definition, types, antecedents, measurement and outcome. *Paediatrics & Child Health*, *9*(8), 541–545. https://doi.org/10.1093/pch/9.8.541

Borawski, D., Sojda, M., Rychlewska, K., & Wajs, T. (2022). Attached but lonely: Emotional intelligence as a mediator and moderator between attachment styles and loneliness. *International Journal of Environmental Research and Public Health*, *19*(22), 14831. https://doi.org/10.3390/ijerph192214831

Bradberry T. & Greaves J. (2009) Emotional Intelligence 2.0, Talent Smart.

Bretherton, l. (1994). The origins of attachment theory: John Bowlby and Mary Ainsworth. *A Century of Developmental Psychology.*, 431–471. https://doi.org/10.1037/10155-029

Bretherton, I. (1992). The origins of attachment theory: John Bowlby and Mary Ainsworth. *Developmental Psychology*, *28*(5), 759–775. https://doi.org/10.1037/0012-1649.28.5.759

Chen SW, Keglovits M, Devine M, Stark S. Sociodemographic Differences in Respondent Preferences for Survey Formats: Sampling Bias and Potential Threats to External Validity. Arch Rehabil Res Clin Transl. 2021 Dec

13;4(1):100175. doi:
10.1016/j.arrct.2021.100175. PMID: 35282151;
PMCID: PMC8904875.

Collins, N. L. (1996). Working models of attachment:
Implications for explanation, emotion, and
behavior. Journal of Personality and Social
Psychology, 71, 810-832.

Collins, N. L., & Read, S. J. (1990). Adult attachment,
working models, and relationship quality in
dating couples. Journal of Personality and Social
Psychology, 54, 644-663.

Collins, N. L. (1996a). Working models of attachment:
Implications for explanation, emotion, and
behavior. *Journal of Personality and Social
Psychology, 71*(4), 810–832.
https://doi.org/10.1037/0022-3514.71.4.810

Collins, N. L. (1996b). Working models of attachment:
Implications for explanation, emotion, and
behavior. *Journal of Personality and Social
Psychology, 71*(4), 810–832.
https://doi.org/10.1037/0022-3514.71.4.810

Collins, N. L., & Read, S. J. (1990). Adult attachment,
working models, and relationship quality in
dating couples. *Journal of Personality and
Social Psychology, 58*(4), 644–663.
https://doi.org/10.1037/0022-3514.58.4.644

Dawda, R., & Hart, S. D. (2000). Assessing emotional
intelligence: Reliability and validity of the
Bar-On Emotional Quotient Inventory (EQ-I) in
university students. Journal of
Personality and individual Differences, 28, 79

Diehl, S. (n.d.). *An Exploratory Study of Attachment Styles and Their Relationship to Emotional Intelligence in a Young Adult Population.* https://doi.org/10.23860/thesis-diehl-steven1998

Doktorová, D., Mičková, Z., & Michal, M. (2020). Determining connections between attachments in romantic relationships and emotional intelligence in female university students. Journal of Education, Society and Behavioural Science, 27-33. https://doi.org/10.9734/jesbs/2020/v33i730241

Elizabeth, S. K., & Wolff, S. B. (2008). Emotional intelligence competencies in the team and team leader: A multi-level examination of the impact of emotional intelligence on team performance. *The Journal of Management Development, 27*(1), 55-75. https://0624fuzqamp03-y-https-doi-org.prx-keiser.lirn.net/10.1108/02621710810840767

Emotional Intelligence Among Selected College Students Amidst the COVID-19 Pandemic. International Journal of Science and Healthcare Research. Vol. 8; Issue: 1; Jan.-March 2023 Website: ijshr.com. ISSN: 2455-7587. DOI: https://doi.org/10.52403/ijshr.20230108

Endler, N. S., & Parker, J. D. A. (1990). Coping Inventory for stressful Situations (CISS): Manual. Toronto, Canada: Multi-Health Systems.

Fabella T., F. E., & N. Litao, D. M. (2023). The relationship between attachment styles and emotional intelligence among selected college students amidst the COVID-19 pandemic. *International Journal of Science and Healthcare Research, 8*(1), 80–89. https://doi.org/10.52403/ijshr.20230108

Gardner, H. (1983). *Frames of mind: The Theory of multiple intelligence.* NYC Basic books.

Gardner, H., Konhaber, M., & Wake, W. (1983). *Intelligence: Multiple perspective.* Harcourt Brace College.

Gardner, H. (2013). Frequently asked questions—Multiple intelligences and related educational topics. https://howardgardner01.files.wordpress.com/2012/06/faq

Greenspan, S, (1989). *The Development of the Ego: Implications for Personality Theory, Psychopathology, and the Psychotherapeutic Process.* International Universities Press

Griffin, D W, & Bartholomew, K. (1994). The metaphysics of measurement: The case of adult attachment. *Advances in personal relationships: attachment processes in adult relationships.* essay, London: Jessica Kingsley.

Griffin, D., & Batholomew, K. (1994). Models of self and other: Fundamental dimensions underlying measures of adult attachment. *Journal of Personality and Social Psychology,* 67, 430-445. https://doi.org/10.1037/0022-3514.67.3.430

Guerra-Bustamante, J., León-del-Barco, B., Yuste-Tosina, R., López-Ramos, V., M., & Mendo-Lázaro, S. (2019). Emotional Intelligence and Psychological Well-Being Adolescents.

International Journal of Environmental Research and Public Health, 16(10) https://0624todb8-mp01-y-https-doi-org.prx-keiser.lirn.net/10.3390/ ijerph16101720

Hamarta, E., Deniz, M. E., & Saltali, N. (2009). Attachment Styles as a Predictor of Emotional Intelligence. *Kuram Ve Uygulamada Egitim Bilimleri, 9*(1), 213-229. https://0624sknkqmp01-y-https-www-proquest-com.prx-keiser.lirn.net/scholarly-journals/attachmentstyles-as-predictor-emotional/docview/237014557/se-2

Handley MA, Lyles CR, McCulloch C, Cattamanchi A. Selecting and Improving QuasiExperimental Designs in Effectiveness and Implementation Research. Annu Rev Public Health. 2018 Apr 1; 39:5-25. doi: 10.1146/annurev-publhealth-040617-014128. Epub 2018 Jan 12. PMID: 29328873; PMCID: PMC8011057.

Henner, T. (1998) Comparing EQ-I and TMMS scale scores unpublished manuscript. Cited in Bar-On, R. (2000). Emotional and social intelligence: Insights from the Emotional Quotient Inventory, In R. Bar-On & J.D.A. Parker (Eds.), The Handbook of Emotional Intelligence (pp. 363-388). San Francisco: Jossey-Bass.

Howard Gardner. frequently asked questions-multiple intelligences and related educational topics. (n.d.).

https://howardgardner01.files.wordpress.com/20
12/06/faq_march2013.pdf

Henner, T. (1998). Comparing EQ-I and TMMS scale
scores. Unpublished manuscript.

İmamoğlu, B. (2022). Between Bureaucratic Tradition
and Professional Discourse: Turkey and the
Case of SİSAG, 1969–77. *Architectural History,
65*, 61-80. https://0624czn18-mp03y-https-doi-
org.prx-keiser.lirn.net/10.1017/arh.2022.4

Jiménez Ballester, A. M., de la Barreera, U., Schoeps,
K., & Montoya-Castilla, I. (2022). Emotional
factors that mediate the relationship between
emotional intelligence and psychological
problems in emerging adults. *Behavioral
Psychology/Psicología
Conductual, 30*(1), 249–267.
https://doi.org/10.51668/bp.8322113n

Johnson, S. (2019). Attachment Theory in Practice:
Emotionally Focused Therapy (EFT) with
Individuals, Couples, and Families. The
Guilford Press, New York.

Khan, A., & Kamal, A. (2023). Emotional Intelligence
as a Mediator between Psychological
Maladjustment and Attachment Styles among
Orphan Adolescents. *Journal of Behavioural
Sciences, 33*(1), 69. https://0624todb8-mp01-y-
https-www-proquestcom.prx-
keiser.lirn.net/scholarly-journals/emotional-
intelligence-as-mediator-between/
docview/2803262101/se-2

Koçoglu, M. (2014). Cynicism as a Mediator of
Relations between Job Stress and Work

Alienation: A Study from a Developing Country
- Turkey. *Global Business and
Management Research, 6*(1), 24-36.
https://0624czn18-mp03-y-https-www-
proquestcom.prx-keiser.lirn.net/scholarly-
journals/cynicism-as-mediator-relations-
between-jobstress/docview/1552829366/se-2

Legacy Place Society. Emotional Intelligence
Significance.
https://legacyplacesociety.com/emotional-
intelligence-
significance/#:~:text=All%20people%20experie
nce%20emotions%2C%20but,irrational%20choi
ces%20and%20counterproductive%20actions.

Lund Research LTD. (2012). Laerd Dissertation.
https://dissertation.laerd.com/processstage6.php

MacCann C., Roberts R. D. (2008). New paradigms for
assessing emotional intelligence: theory and
data. *Emotion* 8, 540–551. 10.1037/a0012746

Maslow, A. H. (1954). *Motivation and personality* (First
ed.). Harper & Row. ISBN 978-0-06-
041987-5.

Mayer J. D., Salovey P., Caruso D. R. (2002a). *Mayer-
Salovey-Caruso Emotional Intelligence
Test (MSCEIT) Item Booklet.* Toronto, ON:
MHS Publishers.

Mayer J. D., Salovey P., Caruso D. R. (2002b). *Mayer-
Salovey-Caruso Emotional Intelligence --
Test (MSCEIT) User's Manual.* Toronto, ON:
MHS Publishers.

Mayer, J. D., Salovey, P., & Caruso, D. R. (2004).
Target articles: "Emotional intelligence:

Theory, findings, and implications."
Psychological Inquiry, 15(3), 197–215.
https://doi.org/10.1207/s15327965pli1503_02

Mcgraw-hill. (1964). Sensitivity to expression of emotional meaning in three modes of communication. In *The communication of emotional meaning.* essay.

McGinley, M., & Evans, A. M. (2020). Parent and/or Peer Attachment? Predicting Emerging Adults' Prosocial Behaviors and Internalizing Symptomatology. *Journal of Child and Family Studies, 29*(7), 1833-1844. https://0624tnadf-mp03-y-https-doi-org.prxkeiser.lirn.net/10.1007/s10826-020-01715-3

Miljkovitch R., Mallet, P., Moss, E., Aino, S., Pascuzzo, K., & Zdebik, M. A. (2021). Adolescents' Attachment to Parents and Peers: Links to Young Adulthood Friendship Quality. *Journal of Child and Family Studies, 30*(6), 1441-1452. https://0624tnadfmp03-y-https-doi-org.prx-keiser.lirn.net/10.1007/s10826-021-01962-y

Mittal, E. ., & Rani, T. (2022). Association Between Secure Attachment Style and Subjective Well-being: Examining the sequential mediation effects . *Asia Pacific Journal of Health Management, 17*(2). https://doi.org/10.24083/apjhm.v17i2.1549

Multi-Health System (MHS), EQ-I 2.0, https://cdn.mhs.com/mhsdocs/EQi20Manual/part1/Intro.html

Murphy, K. R. (Ed.). (2006). A critique of emotional intelligence: What are the problems and how can they be fixed? *Lawrence Erlbaum Associates Publishers.*

National Institute of Mental Health. (2017). Mental Illness. https://www.nimh.nih.gov/health/statistics/mental-illness

O'Connor, P., Hill, A., Kaya, M., Martin, B. (2019). The Measurement of Emotional Intelligence: A Critical Review of the Literature and Recommendations for Researchers and Practitioners. Frontiers in Psychology. VOLUME=10 URL=https://www.frontiersin.org/articles/10.3389/fpsyg.2019.01116. DOI=10.3389/fpsyg.2019.01116. ISSN=1664-1078

Obeid S, Haddad C, Akel M, Fares K, Salameh P, Hallit S. (2019). Factors associated with the adults' attachment styles in Lebanon: The role of alexithymia, depression, anxiety, stress, burnout, and emotional intelligence. Perspect Psychiatr Care. 55(4):607-617. doi: 10.1111/ppc.12379.

Omrod, J. E. 2012. Human Learning. Pearson Education, Inc.

Oxford Dictionary, 2023 Oxford University Press.

Oxford English Dictionary (oed.com)

Parker, J. D. A. (1999). An emotional Stroop task examination of the EQ-i. Unpublished Manuscript.

Parker, J.D.A., Taylor, G.J., & Bagby, R. M. (Forthcoming). The relationship between emotional intelligence and alexithymia. Journal of Personality and Individual Differences.

Petrides K. V., Furnham A. (2001). Trait emotional intelligence: psychometric investigation with reference to established trait taxonomies. *Eur. J. Person.* 15, 425–448. 10.1002/per.416

Phang, A., Fan, W., and Arbona, C. (2020). Secure attachment and career indecision: the mediating role of emotional intelligence. *J. Career Dev.* 47, 657–670. doi: 10.1177/0894845318814366

Salguero, J.M.; Fernández-Berrocal, P.; Ruiz-Aranda, D.; Castillo, R.; Palomera, R. Inteligencia emocional y ajuste psicosocial en la adolescencia: El papel de la percepción emocional (Emotional intelligence and psychological and social adjustment in adolescence: The role of emotional perception). *Eur. J. Educ. Psychol.* 2015, *4*, 142-153.

Salovey, P., & Mayer, J. D. (1990). Emotional intelligence. *Imagination, Cognition and Personality*, 9(3), 185–211.

Scarlat, E. (2021). The role of cognitive schemas in the relationship between attachment style and emotional intelligence. *Studia Doctoralia* 54(69) 12. 10.47040/sd/sdpsych.v12i1.123

Schutte N. S., Malouff J. M., Hall L. E., Haggerty D. J., Cooper J. T., Golden C. J., et al. (1998). Development and validation of a measure of emotional intelligence. *Personal.*

Indivi. Diff. 25, 167–177. 10.1016/S0191-8869(98)00001-4

Seligman, M.E.P., Abramson, L. Y., Semmel, A., & Von Baeyer, C. (1979). Depressive attributional style. Journal of Abnormal Psychology, 88, 242-247.

Sfetcu, N. (2020). Critique of Emotional Intelligence in Organizations. 10.13140/RG.2.2.17749.04329

Shen, F., Liu, Y., & Brat, M. (2021). Attachment, Self-Esteem, and Psychological Distress: A Multiple-Mediator Model. *The Professional Counselor, 11*(2), 129-142. https://0624tnadf-mp03-y-https-doi-org.prx-keiser.lirn.net/10.15241/fs.11.2.129

Simpson, J. A., Rholes, S. W., & Phillips, D. (1996). Conflict in close relationships: An attachment perspective. Journal of Personality and Social Psychology, 71, 899-914. doi: 10.1037/0022-3514.71.5.899

Ştefan, C. & Avram, J. (2019). Investigating Attachment Status Effects on Preschoolers' Empathic Perspective-Taking. *Child & Youth Care Forum, 48*(5), 663-675. https://0624tnadf-mp03-y-https-doi-org.prx-keiser.lirn.net/10.1007/s10566-019-09498-5

Stubbs Koman, E., & Wolff, S. B. (2008). Emotional intelligence competencies in the team and team leader. *Journal of Management Development, 27*(1), 55–75. https://doi.org/10.1108/02621710810840767

Svensson, H. (2011). Attachment dimensions as a
        predictor of emotional intelligence and
        sociability. *PsycEXTRA Dataset.*
        https://doi.org/10.1037/e530162013-001
The attachment project. (2023). Learn attachment
theory from experts. Attachment Project.
http://www.attachmentproject.com/
The Emotional Intelligence Training Company Inc.
2023. Assess your emotional intelligence,
        EQ-i 2.0/EQ 360 | The Emotional Intelligence
        Training Company
        (eitrainingcompany.com)
The Origins of Emotional Intelligence Theory. (2020).
        https://impellus.com/wp-
        content/uploads/2020/06/Emotional-
        Intelligence-backgroundreading.pdf
The Myers-Briggs Company. 2023. EQ-i 2.0® and EQ
        360® Emotional
        Intelligence Assessment for Leadership
        ap.themyersbriggs.com/overview/EQ-i-20-8
Wei-Wen, C., Gao, X., Wang, Z., & Mak Miranda, C. K.
        (2022). Unhappy us, unhappy me, unhappy life:
        The role of self-esteem in the relation between
        adult attachment styles and mental health:
        Research and Reviews. *Current Psychology,
        41*(2), 837-846.
        https://0624tnadf-mp03-y-https-doi-org.prx-
        keiser.lirn.net/10.1007/s12144-019-00594-2
West, M., Rose, M. S., & Sheldon-Keller, A.
        (1994). Assessment of patterns of insecure
        attachment in adults and application to
        dependent and schizoid personality

disorders. *Journal of Personality Disorders*, 8(3), 249-256.

Yahya F., Ghazali N. M., Anuar A., Othman M. R. (2019)._Adult Attachment and Emotional Intelligence. International Journal of Engineering and Technology 8(1S):123-134

Zvara, Bharathi & Lathren, Christine & Mills-Koonce, William & Contributors, the. (2020). Maternal and Paternal Attachment Style and Chaos as Risk Factors for Parenting Behavior. Family Relations. 69. 10.1111/fare.12423.

.

Appendix A

Relationship Scale Questionnaire

Please read each of the following statements
and rate the extent to
  which you believe each statement best
  describes your feelings
  about a close relationship.
1. Top of Form
   1.I find it difficult to depend on
   other people.
   a. Not at all like me
   b. Not like me
   c. Somewhat like me
   d. Like me
   e. Very much like me

2. It is very important to me to feel
   independent.
   a. Not at all like me
   b. Not like me
   c. Somewhat like me
   d. Like me
   e. Very much like me

3. I find it easy to get emotionally
   close to others.
   a. Not at all like me
   b. Not like me
   c. Somewhat like me
   d. Like me

e.   Very much like me
4.   I want to merge completely with
another person.
    a.   Not at all like me
    b.   Not like me
    c.   Somewhat like me
    d.   Like me
    e.   Very much like me

5.   I worry that I will be hurt if I allow
myself to become too
close to others.
    a.   Not at all like me
    b.   Not like me
    c.   Somewhat like me
    d.   Like me
    e.   Very much like me

6.   I am comfortable without close
emotional relationships.
    a.   Not at all like me
    b.   Not like me
    c.   Somewhat like me
    d.   Like me
    e.   Very much like me

7.   I am not sure that I can always
depend on others to be there
when I need them.
    a.   Not at all like me
    b.   Not like me

    c.   Somewhat like me
    d.   Like me
    e.   Very much like me

8. I want to be completely emotionally intimate with others.
    a.   Not at all like me
    b.   Not like me
    c.   Somewhat like me
    d.   Like me
    e.   Very much like me

9. I worry about being alone.
    a.   Not at all like me
    b.   Not like me
    c.   Somewhat like me
    d.   Like me
    e.   Very much like me

10. I am comfortable depending on other people.
    a.   Not at all like me
    b.   Not like me
    c.   Somewhat like me
    d.   Like me
    e.   Very much like me

11. I often worry that romantic partners don't love me.
    a.   Not at all like me
    b.   Not like me

c. Somewhat like me
d. Like me
e. Very much like me

12. I find it difficult to trust others completely.
    a. Not at all like me
    b. Not like me
    c. Somewhat like me
    d. Like me
    e. Very much like me

13. I worry about others getting too close to me.
    a. Not at all like me
    b. Not like me
    c. Somewhat like me
    d. Like me
    e. Very much like me

14. I want emotionally close relationships.
    a. Not at all like me
    b. Not like me
    c. Somewhat like me
    d. Like me
    e. Very much like me

15. I am comfortable having other people depend on me.
    a. Not at all like me

b. Not like me

c. Somewhat like me

d. Like me

e. Very much like me

16. I worry that others don't value me
as much as I value them.

a. Not at all like me

b. Not like me

c. Somewhat like me

d. Like me

e. Very much like me

17. People are never there when you
need them.

a. Not at all like me

b. Not like me

c. Somewhat like me

d. Like me

e. Very much like me

18. My desire to merge completely
sometimes scares people away.

a. Not at all like me

b. Not like me

c. Somewhat like me

d. Like me

e. Very much like me

19. It is very important to me to feel
self-sufficient.

a. Not at all like me

b. Not like me
c. Somewhat like me
d. Like me
e. Very much like me

20. I am nervous when anyone gets too close to me.
    a. Not at all like me
    b. Not like me
    c. Somewhat like me
    d. Like me
    e. Very much like me

21. I often worry that romantic partners won't want to stay with me.
    a. Not at all like me
    b. Not like me
    c. Somewhat like me
    d. Like me
    e. Very much like me

22. I prefer not to have other people depend on me.
    a. Not at all like me
    b. Not like me
    c. Somewhat like me
    d. Like me
    e. Very much like me

23. I worry about being abandoned.
    a. Not at all like me

b. Not like me

c. Somewhat like me

d. Like me

e. Very much like me

24. I am somewhat uncomfortable being close to others.

    a. Not at all like me

    b. Not like me

    c. Somewhat like me

    d. Like me

    e. Very much like me

25. I find that others are reluctant to get as close as I would like.

    a. Not at all like me

    b. Not like me

    c. Somewhat like me

    d. Like me

    e. Very much like me

26. I prefer not to depend on others.

    a. Not at all like me

    b. Not like me

    c. Somewhat like me

    d. Like me

    e. Very much like me

27. I know that others will be there when I need them.

    a. Not at all like me

b. Not like me
c. Somewhat like me
d. Like me
e. Very much like me

28. I worry about having others not
accept me.
a. Not at all like me
b. Not like me
c. Somewhat like me
d. Like me
e. Very much like me

29. Romantic partners often want me to
be closer than I
feel comfortable being.
a. Not at all like me
b. Not like me
c. Somewhat like me
d. Like me
e. Very much like me

30. I find it relatively easy to get close
to others.
a. Not at all like me
b. Not like me
c. Somewhat like me
d. Like me
e. Very much like me

SCORE CARD INSTRUCTION
The secure attachment style
included items 3,9,10, 15,
and 28; the fearful/avoidance
attachment style included
items 1, 5, 12, and 24. The
preoccupied attachment style
included items 6, 8, 16, and 25; and
the dismissing
attachment style included items 2,
6, 19, 22 and 26.
Reverse scoring was computed for
items 9, 28, and 6
(Grifin & Bartholomew,
1994).Bottom of Form

Appendix B

Demographic Questionnaire

The following questions ask you
demographic questions

for classification purposes only.

1. Top of Form
2. How old are you?
3. What is your gender?
    Male
    Female
    Gender variant/non-conforming
    Other (please specify)
4. What is your ethnicity?
    Hispanic
    Not Hispanic
    Prefer not to answer
    Other (please specify)
5. What is your race?
    White
    Black or African American
    Hispanic or Latino
    Asian or Asian American
    American Indian or Alaska
    Native
    Native Hawaiian or other
    Pacific Islander
    Mixed race
    Other (please specify)

6. What is your current education
    level?
    Associate Degree
    Bachelor's Degree
    Master's Degree
    Doctorate Degree
    Other (please specify)
7. Are you currently enrolled in
    university, college, or
    trade school classes?
    Part Time
    Full Time
    Not at all
    Prefer not to answer
8. Are you currently working for
    pay?
    Part Time
    Full Time
    Not at all
    Prefer not to answer
9. Please select the option that best
    represents your family
    structure growing up.
    Nuclear Family: living with
    both biological parents
    Single Parent Family: living
    with only one biological parent
    Stepparent Family: living with
    one biological and
    one non-biological parent

Extended Family: living with
family that extends
beyond parents ex: grandparent,
aunt, uncle etc.
Grandparent Family: living with
grandparents who
 are the sole caregivers.
Unconventional Family: all
other family types,
 like same-sex family, adopted
parents, foster parents, etc.
10. In what state or U.S. territory
do you live?

Appendix C

Emotional intelligence Questionaire:
Samples

I'm aware of how others feel.

I see situations as they really are.

I cling to others.

I pay attention to how I'm feeling.

I try to make a difference in society.

I like helping people.

I enjoy talking to people.

I am empathic.

I can't think clearly when I'm under stress.

I am not happy with my life.

I am good at understanding the way other people feel.

I am optimistic.

My impulsiveness creates problems for me.

Recruitment

Online Research Collection

https://psych.hanover.edu/research/exponnet.html

Does Attachment Style Predict Emotional

Intelligence in College Students in the U.S. Population? Click here to participate!

EMAIL

Hello Potential Participants,

My name is Titilola Ologbonjaiye, and I am a doctoral candidate in industrial and organizational psychology at Keiser University. For my dissertation, I am investigating the relationship between attachment style and emotional intelligence among college students. I am inviting you to participate in this exciting research. By completing two surveys, you will contribute to advancing psychological knowledge and have a chance to win a $ 25 Amazon gift card. Additionally, you will receive a $5 gift card upon completing both surveys. If you have any questions, please contact me at T.Ologbonjaiye@student.keiseruniversity.edu. The link to the study is located below. Please begin with the first survey, which will lead to the second survey. https://www.surveymonkey.com/r/6BS7GMJ

Thank you in advance.
Titilola Ologbonjaiye

EMAIL By Other Recruiters

Hello Potential Participants, College students are invited to participate in the research "Attachment Style as a Predictor of Emotional Intelligence in a U.S. Population." Participation involves completing two surveys. If you choose to participate and complete both surveys, you will receive a $5 gift card and enter a drawing to win one of four $25 Amazon gift cards. If you have any questions regarding this study, don't hesitate to contact T.Ologbonjaiye@student.keiseruniversity.edu. The survey link is below. Please begin with the first survey, which will lead to the second survey. https://www.surveymonkey.com/r/6BS7GMJ

Thank you!

Instagram, LinkedIn, and Facebook.

Participate in the research titled Attachment Style as a Predictor of Emotional Intelligence in a U.S. Population. Participation requires the completion of two surveys. If you choose to participate and complete both surveys, you will receive a $5 gift card and enter a drawing to win 1 of 4 $25 Amazon gift cards. If you have any questions regarding this study, please contact T.Ologbonjaiye@student.keiseruniversity.edu. The survey link is below. Please begin with the first survey, which will lead to the second survey.
https://www.survey=monkey.com/r/6BS7GMJ